The Cosmic
Crystal Spiral

Born in America in 1944, Ra Bonewitz trained and
worked as a geologist. A visit to the Findhorn com-
munity in Scotland in 1977 changed the direction of his
life and helped him to discover his latent gifts as a trance
medium and healer. He gave up a lucrative job in the oil
industry and travelled widely giving lectures and workshops on crystal energies. He now lives in London and
works as a personal and business consultant.

The Cosmic Crystal Spiral

*Crystals and the Evolution of
Human Consciousness*

Ra Bonewitz

Element Books

© Ra Bonewitz 1986
First published in Great Britain in 1986 by
Element Books Ltd,
Longmead, Shaftesbury,
Dorset

Second impression 1987

Typeset in Linotron Palatino by
Characters, Taunton, Somerset
Printed in Great Britain by
Billings, Hylton Road, Worcester
Text designed by Humphrey Stone
Cover illustration by Tad Mann

British Library Cataloguing in Publication Data
Bonewitz, Ra
The cosmic crystal spiral: crystals and
the evolution of human consciousness.
1. Crystals   2. Occult sciences
I. Title
133   BF1442.C7

ISBN 0-906540-94-1

Contents

to

ANNIE LOCKE

*whose inner beauty dims
the finest gem*

Introduction

This is a book about you – who you are, what you are, what you have been, how you became it, and what you might possibly continue to be. It is not a cookbook; a book about 'how to do it better with crystals'. Nor is it a book for those who think that crystals are the be all and end all of everything. If you believe that it is possible to change the world around you without first changing yourself, then read no further as this book is not for you.

This book will not make you richer or poorer, it will not make you better looking, it won't make you any taller or sexier, nor will it grow hair in the bald spots. But what you *can* learn from this book is a different way of seeing yourself, and as a consequence, the world around you.

Life is all a matter of perspectives. This book is based entirely on one concept – *what you see, depends on where you stand.*

A short while back, I took a personal development course which was very important to my own inner awakening.

At the completion of the course, we were asked to visualize all the people in our lifetime with whom we had had conflict or deep emotional experiences, or who had created tremendous difficulties for us. This was an exercise in forgiveness, and we were asked to visualize all the people we wished to forgive, and the experiences that created the need for forgiveness. Then we were asked to see all of the completed emotional energies as rubbish on the floor, which we were then to sweep up and put into plastic bags. The next part of the exercise was to visualize ourselves as rocketships taking those worn out emotional energies and returning them to the Cosmos.

What hit me was that all of this muck was the energy that

has powered my lifetime, the rocket fuel, the energy to power my own 'rocket' of self, propelling me back to the stars, back to reunion with my true self.

Since then I have also come to realize that the little quirks of my personality (come to think of it, some of them aren't so little) which I have often considered a burden, when seen from another point of view, are the gifts I have given myself to propel me into a new understanding.

Here is a simple example: if I were still a conventional thinker, I would have never delved into the questions about life and the Universe that have led to this book. Through the search for answers to these larger questions, I have found a broader acceptance of who and what I am, and a different way of seeing my own weaknesses which, when seen from an entirely different perspective, are my greatest strengths. *What you see, depends on where you stand.*

A great deal of what you will be reading in this book could loosely be put under the heading of 'science'. But as I have already said that this is a book about perspectives, let me give you another perspective of the word science. *Science is the branch of mysticism that deals with the measurable.* We could invert that definition if we wish, and say with equal truth that *mysticism is the branch of science that deals with the unmeasurable.*

There is a fundamental spiritual law that says "as above, so below". What does this mean exactly? It is saying that as we observe an activity at one level of being, say at the material level, we will find exact correspondence in other levels of energy, even in those unmeasurable levels of energy that we call 'spirit'. We are looking at a spectrum of energy.

It also says that the one difference between the levels of energy that we call 'science' and the levels of energy that we call 'mysticism', is our ability to measure. In my courses, I have often said that something exists to a scientist, only if you can measure it, and paint it green. This is a bit tongue in cheek, and not quite so true with modern physics, yet it doesn't miss the mark by far with scientific traditionalists. You might have also noticed that this arbitrary division between measurable and unmeasurable is mostly created in the mind. It depends totally on 'where you stand'.

But this trend, at last, is changing in the 'hard' sciences – physics, chemistry, etc. I recently saw a panel discussion with a nuclear physicist, a microbiologist and a neurosurgeon. The word that kept cropping up with some excitement in the discussion was 'holism' – as if it were some newly discovered key to the Universe. Thank goodness physics has finally found it. The mystics are on written record for at least 3,000 years as saying "it's all energy" – at last science is catching up!

What we are discovering in nuclear physics is what I hope to underline strongly in this book: all we are dealing with wherever we live in the Universe is just different levels of energy, some of which is unmanifest at one extreme, called spirit, and some of which we find at the other extreme in a manifest form which we call matter. Because it is *all* energy, and all energy obeys a few basic laws. They are called the laws of physics in science, and called spiritual law in esoterics – everything in the Universe obeys *exactly the same laws*. The way we see and experience them simply depends on our perspective. *What you see, depends on where you stand.*

I hope what you discover about yourself in this book will give you a new place to stand.

Many blessings,
RA BONEWITZ
LONDON, 1986

1

Chaos

This is a book about patterns. All things in the Universe create patterns – patterns of atoms, patterns of cells, patterns of behaviour, patterns of relationships.

As we examine these patterns a new pattern begins to emerge, the pattern of existence that is you and me.

The book is constructed around the subject of crystals – fundamental patterns in themselves. But we cannot separate them as if they exist in isolation. They are only part, albeit an integral part, of a greater pattern, the ongoing flow of creation that is the Universe.

Throughout my own search for Self, I have been gifted with certain insights, which, for me, serve to reflect back to me, who I am. Most of you know this is how the world works anyway. Everything we see in the world is only a projection of Self. Because my own pattern has created in me an early life where I wished to avoid living in this world at all cost, I felt forced to look into other worlds. I didn't know that at the time of course; I thought I was just introspective.

From my scientific training, I have managed to avoid certain of the pitfalls of such an inner search, where illusions lurk to pounce on the unwary. Other pitfalls I have leapt into with both eyes wide open – and unseeing. Years ago I used to tell my flying students: "When you have made all the mistakes, you know all the answers." I've certainly had a personal experience of that!

The word God will be used a lot in this book, so here is my definition: *God is all that exists, manifest and unmanifest*. I believe that God and the Universe are the same thing; not just the Universe as a few galaxies and stars, but the Universe as a field of energy, including the energy of consciousness. The following chapters will expand this definition.

There is a lot of 'science' early on in this book, but I've tried to keep it simple for those of you without a science background. Please bear with it, as the information is important to anchor the more interpretive parts of the book.

I have hopes that many people from the 'science' side of the measurement dividing line will also read this. For you, the factual information may be a bit thin but at least you can see the sources of the new ideas presented herein. A lot of the interpretations would be pretty hard to 'prove' scientifically.

Here's a clue: somewhere inside of you is a feeling you get when something is true, or likewise when it is not. That feeling you get when something 'rings true'. We all have it.

Take a moment before you read on to remember how it feels for you, this 'ring of truth'. As you read, run all that you read through your own *inner sense of truth*.

There are, by the way, no ultimate truths. As we will discover, the Universe is an unfinished place, so what is true in one moment, may not be true in the next. All you can discover is what is true *for you*. It may not be true for anyone else. Because no two of us occupy the same space (physically), nor do any two of us have identical experiences (which is the looking glass through which we see the world, and thus ourselves), it is *impossible* for any two people to see *anything* in exactly the same way. This is the basis for your own uniqueness in the Universe.

So what is this Universe we live in, or more correctly, are part of? And why a Universe anyway?

Here is a question for you: if God is all things that exist, why does He need to create a Universe in the first place?

And if there is a reason for the creation of the Universe, then why did God need to put *you* in it?

The answer to these questions is really what this book is all about.

It is a book about relationships. Not man-woman, as we traditionally use the term, but relationships between things. We have a usual view of the Universe as being made of 'things' – stars, planets, atoms, carrots, doorknobs.

I have a different view.

I see the Universe as being made of *relationships*. These relationships have a physical outworking as *things*, as matter, but if there were no relationships, no matter would exist.

Because we are in the habit of seeing things as separate objects rather than relationships, I will work from that viewpoint – how a 'thing' came into being, and then look at the relationship that caused it.

A brief example before we begin: most of you know by now that your physical body and its state of being are a direct result of your own inner energy patterns. When blockages occur in your own energy flow, physical illness results. In other words, the state of your physical health is a result of your own inner energy relationships.

If your own body is a result of certain states of energy, why should the body of the Universe be any different? Don't we say often enough that man is the microcosm of the Universe?

We now know with absolute certainty that the Universe and all in it are made from *energy*. We know now in physics that matter is just another state of energy. It is *all energy*.

But energy in different levels of *relationship*. Energy on one relationship level is called an electron – on another level or type of relationship it is a photon, etc. Then these basic particles enter into a more complex relationship called atoms – and atoms into deeper relationships called crystals, and so on to build planets, and people, and cheeseburgers.

So where did all begin?

In the beginning, there *was* a beginning. The Universe *began*. Which also implies there was a time when the Universe *wasn't*. And if it wasn't, what wasn't it?

The answer to that, of course, is what it is!

Take a minute to reflect on that, because you can substitute the word 'you' for the word 'Universe'.

You began. *You* weren't. *You* are.

You and the Universe came into being at exactly the same instant. Every bit of energy that makes up YOU was part of that first instant of Universal birth.

Fifteen thousand million years ago.

Is it any wonder we feel so *old* on Monday mornings!

All that you are, all that you have ever been, and all that you will ever be was there in that first moment. What you are now is a direct out-growth of those first seconds in which the Universe came into being. You were there. Of course not in the form that you exist in now, but every speck of energy that makes up your physical body, your mental, emotional and spiritual bodies, was all there, in that moment.

The root of your being is the same root as all that lives in the Universe.

And the Universe itself.

Energetically, your roots are the same as the stars and the planets, the moon and comets, the galaxies, the nebulae, everything.

Scientists and mystics are in agreement at last. In the beginning it was all energy (mystics often use the words vibration, or light).

How 'long' the Universe was in this state of pure energy is difficult to say.

Let's pause for a moment, and look at the question of time, as implied by the word 'long'. We have lived in a world so used to dividing the hours of daylight and darkness into segments, that we have come to believe 'time' is something that actually exists, exists in the same sort of physical sense as wrist-watches or cabbages. And yet, our concept of time is mostly an artificial invention, and is entirely dependent on the perception of the person who measures it.

Time is our experience of movement. The ageing of our bodies (movement of cells), our movement from place to place, the movement of astronomical bodies. For example: at 8 a.m. (the position of the Sun relative to the rotation of the Earth), I leave for work (move my position from my home to my workplace).

Time may be connected with the interplanetary forces that we call Astrology. Einstein gives us formulae relating mass, time, and speed. A few simple computations will show us that massive objects, such as planets, travelling at different speeds, will produce different rates of time passage. In other words, 'time' is different on each planet in the solar system. Because time varies from planet to planet, the space between the planets must distort to accommodate. I am certain that these distortions of space/time influence the human organism (or all organisms for that matter), and that Astrology, especially removed from its 'fortune telling' aspect, may well have some validity.

One of the basics of Einsteinian physics is the question of time; the fundamental view is that time is all relative to the person who observes it.

You have probably had your own experience of the relativity of time. For example, how long does five minutes pass when you are with a lover? Or, how quickly does five minutes pass when you are stuck in a traffic jam, and late for an appointment? Or, how quickly do you suppose five minutes would pass if you were sitting on a hot stove? Likewise, many of you have experienced *timelessness* in the meditative state. Have you ever been in a meditative space where it feels like only a short time has passed, yet when you return to outer awareness perhaps an hour has gone by? Truly, the state of meditation is nearer the pure energy sense than any outer experience of time in the physical world, and therefore we might expect it to be closer to the Universe's experience of time in its pure energy state. So, if the Universe were only in a pure energy state for a matter of seconds, at least according to our concept of a few seconds, it may well have seemed like forever in the Universe's experience of itself.

But does the Universe itself experience? And, does it experience itself?

These are questions vital to the meaning of all life, and to me at least, to the meaning of *my* life. They may be to yours too. What I have found for myself about these questions, I will share in Chapter Seven.

These are questions about *why*. For the moment, I'd like to stick to *how*. I don't know about you, but I have often found that if I look at a thing from several different perspectives, the why becomes part of the how.

So how *did* it happen?

In the beginning the Universe was in a pure state of energy, formless, in a pure state of chaos. As we live in a world of form, and the Universe, as we shall discover in this book, is moving into greater and greater complexity of form and higher states of order, this formless state represents the highest state of disorder – chaos.

But somewhere in this disordered state, there was the germ of an idea. Perhaps not a conscious idea in the sense that you and I would sit down and draw out plans for a house, or work out how to make our pay cheque last to next pay day, but perhaps an inner experience of an idea, an idea that there might be another state of being other than complete disorder.

This may not have been unlike the germ of thought many of us had about our chaotic lives before the 'Spiritual Path'. Is this all there is?

In this state, the Universe may be likened to an unfertilized human ovum, a single human cell. Within the inner nature of that human ovum is an entire human being, and all that that human being will be in its lifetime. Surely at whatever level of consciousness the ovum exists, there must be an awareness that this is so. An awareness that exists at the experience level, rather than at the consciousness or thought level.

The Universe at this state must have been a long way from even the level of consciousness of the Mineral Kingdom, because at the temperatures and pressures being experienced by the Universe at this stage of its creation, solid matter couldn't exist.

Because the physical body is a reflection of the energy state, the consciousness state, this chaotic physical state suggests that even the Universe itself went through an early, chaotic state of consciousness. "Is *this* all there is?" on a cosmic scale. In its pure energy state the Universe was millions of times hotter than the centre of the Sun, and in its 'ovum' state was about the size of a large pea! Imagine: everything that exists in the

Universe, in a sphere this size.

In comic strips, we often illustrate the birth of an idea as a light going on. We also speak of "the light dawning". Perhaps this is a memory of our own original birth, the birth of the Universe.

Because the first idea that the Universe had of itself – to move from energy to matter – would have been a burst of light unlike any seen since. The birth of a star would be a feeble flicker of a candle alongside it.

THE BIG BANG.

The Universe moving from energy to matter. Creating in that first burst of Universal life the four primitive building blocks of atoms: *photons*, light; *neutrinos*, so small they pass right through the Earth without hitting anything; *electrons*, negatively charged particles; and *positrons*, positively charged electrons. With approximately equal amounts of each. Energy moving into a new state of consciousness, an awareness of itself as 'particles'. A new way of relating energy to energy.

In many esoteric writings we read that the Universe and all in it is made from 'light'. If we take the statement literally, we know now that it is not so, that 'light' (photons) makes up about one fourth of the manifest Universe. This is, of course, taking the statement literally. We could restate it: the Universe is made up of energies and forces moving to create higher and higher states of being; these are the forces which we often refer to as the forces of 'light'. Photons are in fact, discovered to be what are called gauge particles, force carriers of electromagnetism.

The Universe in the beginning then, containing you and all that you are, was a great seething mass of energy at a temperature nearing infinite. As the Big Bang began, after about one hundredth of a second, the temperature had cooled to about 100 thousand million degrees centigrade, and certain of the basic particles had begun to condense from the broth of radiation. The Universe as a whole was largely a soup of sub-atomic particles and radiation, and still totally without form or structure.

The Universe was so compact at this stage that even neutrinos, millions of times smaller than an atom, were, at this immensely high density, kept in balance by collisions with themselves, and other particles. The density at this stage would have been approximately 3.8 thousand million times the density of water under normal Earth conditions. A teaspoon of matter at this density would weigh as much as an entire mountain range on Earth.

By the end of the first second a new relationship appeared – the first four particles began to bind themselves into even larger, denser particles, with new particles appearing to 'glue' them together. These were the first protons and neutrons, particles that would eventually form the centres, or nuclei, of atoms although the energies were still far too great for them to be bound together. This event began around ten seconds later, when the Universe had cooled to about 3 thousand million degrees centigrade. This is cool enough for stable nuclei like helium to form, although they were still forming and dissolving back into the 'soup' at a rapid rate. Even at this stage, the Universe was still mostly made of free energy, with a relatively few photons, neutrinos, and anti-neutrinos.

By the time three minutes had passed, the Universe cooled to a thousand million degrees centigrade, 'only' about seventy times hotter than the centre of the Sun.

So, after the first three minutes, the fundamental processes which shaped the early Universe were set in motion, processes which ran for another 700,000 years, to the point where the Universe had cooled sufficiently for electrons to be attracted to atomic nuclei, to begin to form atoms. Hydrogen and some helium were the first products of this new energy relationship.

Your own body develops in a similar manner: first an 'explosion' of cells to set the first stage in motion – the creation of building blocks. Cells for you, particles for the Universe.

For the Universe the process took about three minutes to set in motion (remembering the relativity of time, three minutes may have seemed like lifetimes to those emerging particles).

For you, it is the amount of time it takes the sperm to pass to the ovum its genetic information, and set in motion the energy of the cells to replicate themselves.

A few minutes.

For the Universe to produce atoms – free electrons moving into a new relationship, being bound to atomic nuclei – took 70,000 years. How 'long' this was in the Universe's experience of itself is hard to say. But remember that the larger the physical body (at least in terms of Earth biology), the longer it 'lives'. By this time the Universe had gone from the size of a pea to larger than a galaxy, so perhaps in a body of that size, 70,000 years may have only seemed a few hours.

Our understanding of the atom is growing from our ability to construct machines (called accelerators) that begin to approximate conditions soon after the Big Bang. We will never be able to duplicate it exactly though, short of creating *another* Big Bang. And I don't think many of us are ready for that one yet.

As their name implies, they accelerate particles to incredibly high speeds, and crash them together to break them down into their component parts.

But that has its own problems, as theoretical physicist, Dr Carlo Rubbia recently pointed out:

"It's a bit like finding out how cars work by smashing them together and seeing what falls out.

But in particle physics, when you smash two cars together, you get twenty or thirty new cars, or even a truck or two. We're repeating one of the miracles of the Universe – transforming energy into matter."[1]

But despite the difficulties, a clear picture has begun to emerge. What we now see is that atoms are made up of two

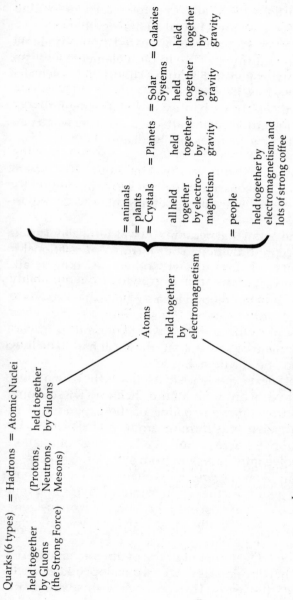

Quarks (6 types) = Hadrons = Atomic Nuclei

held together   (Protons,   held together
by Gluons   Neutrons,   by Gluons
(the Strong Force)   Mesons)

Atoms

held together
by
electromagnetism

= animals
= plants
= Crystals   = Planets   = Solar   = Galaxies
                             Systems

all held   held   held   held
together   together   together   together
by electro-   by   by   by
magnetism   gravity   gravity   gravity

= people

held together by
electromagnetism and
lots of strong coffee

Leptons   = Atomic Outer Shells

Electrons,   held together by Photons
Muons,   (electromagnetism)
Neutrino

held together by
the Weak Force

groups of six particles each, and four force carriers to 'glue' them together. Table 1 shows how it all fits together.

The next state of emerging order appeared at the same time the first atoms were forming. The simplest elements were the first to appear – hydrogen and helium. Almost with a sense of "I'll try this out and see if it works."

Before this time electrons had existed as free agents – no attachments. Being attracted and attached to nuclei was a new relationship, with new energies involved, and also a new commitment.

I'm not saying any of this was reasoned out. This was all pre-ordained by the sequence of events set in motion by the Big Bang. And yet it was still something new to be experienced.

The instant the ovum that became you was fertilized, certain things were also pre-ordained. Your birth, your relationship with your parents, relationships with others, learning to talk, and walk, and so on.

As your life was set in motion by a single, explosive event, so was the life of the Universe.

But although all of those events were guaranteed in your future at the moment of conception, they still had to be lived and experienced one at a time, in order.

The Universe's next experience of itself was the formation of vast clouds of hydrogen, with a bit of helium. These clouds were probably from uneven cooling of the expanding Universe, with the cooler areas forming atoms first. These clouds were millions of miles across, and at a later stage of relationship, would evolve into stars, and from stars into galaxies.

Again, we can liken the processes shaping the newly born Universe to the ovum. As the ovum begins to divide and multiply, what develops is almost entirely dependent on the genetics of the ovum; likewise the early Universe was governed purely by the laws of physics.

Throughout the development of the ovum into an embryo, the only thing that develops is what *can* develop. Likewise, the development of the early Universe went the way it did because it was the only way that it *could* go.

The early Universe was running on 'automatic pilot'.

But it had made its first choice: to incarnate or not to incarnate. As it turns out, this is the first choice that governs the Organic Kingdoms as well.

The quest of the Universe to find *you* had begun.

As the Universe's idea of itself began to take form, order was appearing, although at the microcosmic level of the atom. In the macrocosm, chaos still reigned, although slowly order began to appear.

The areas of the Universe where hydrogen and helium had begun to collect in swirling clouds eventually to become the galaxies, were, within themselves, beginning to take on a slightly higher degree of order. Within these clouds, denser areas began to appear. The faintest forces of gravitation were beginning to operate between individual atoms, and gradually denser and denser areas of hydrogen and helium became attracted to one another through these minute forces. These patches of slightly more compact gas began to attract more and more gas to themselves, increasing the density, thus increasing their gravitational attraction to even more gas. More and more gas was attracted, the clouds became denser and denser, and their interiors began to heat up from the increasing weight and pressure.

By this point we can see the beginning of a Universal process – expansion and contraction. First the expansion of the Universe itself, then a contraction into atoms of hydrogen and helium, with further contraction into dense and compact clouds of gas.

The next cycle of expansion began in the centre of these compact gas clouds – when hydrogen atoms began to fuse together to form more helium, releasing light and more heat in the process.

The first stars burst into life, their light expanding to fill the Universe.

If you could have watched the Universe at this stage it might be rather like sitting on a hilltop at dusk, watching the lights of a great city come on. Across the vast darkness, the very first star would burst into light, followed by a second, and a third beginning to twinkle somewhere in the distance, until at last the Universe was ablaze with light. And somewhere through all of this was everything that makes up You.

The birthing process of stars can be observed even today, for it is an ongoing process. Depending on the part of the world in which you live, you can see a group of stars called The Pleiades, also known as The Seven Sisters, a group of seven stars surrounded by a fuzzy field of light. These are stars now in the process of being born, and the fuzzy cloud around them is the gas cloud from which they are condensing.

In the centres of these first stars, the pattern of star life was being established. The word 'life' is used deliberately, because stars go through the same life processes as you and me – birth, life, death, and rebirth. As the contraction stage to denser helium progressed, the density of the star core caused temperatures to rise even further, to the point where the heliums began to fuse into even denser atoms.

At each stage of fusion, more heat and light is released in an expansion, as the fused atoms contract in density.

Helium fuses into carbon, carbon fuses into oxygen, and by addition through fusion of further heliums in successive stages of expansion and contraction, neon, magnesium, silicon, sulphur, and eventually, iron are created.

Stars, through their life processes, create heavy matter – what you and I are made of.

The very last expansion or contraction of the star will be its own death.

The energy structure of the star will be vastly altered by the fusion process and the amount of light that it has released. Eventually, the star will reach a point where the atomic forces which support its structure become exactly equal to the much weaker gravitational forces that are trying to collapse the star into its own dense centre. In the instant the gravitational force is the stronger of the two, this is exactly what happens: the star violently collapses in a matter of seconds. As the star collapses inwards, only two things can happen. If the star began with more than a certain amount of hydrogen, the amount of matter in the core will cause the collapsing star to 'rebound' and expand outward once again until a new state of balance between density and gravity is reached. At this stage the rebound will carry the remaining hydrogen much further from the centre than the previous stage, and the star will become much cooler. This type of star is called a Red Giant, and such a star may be hundreds or even thousands of times its original diameter. Our own star, the Sun, is such a star, and in its first stage of death will expand to nearly the orbit of the Earth, to become a Red Giant.

Even when expanded the fusion process still continues in the core, creating much more density and releasing more heat and light energy. Such a star then experiences at a later stage, exactly the same sort of gravitational collapse and rebound as in the first stage, although in this final stage, the star continues to expand forever – it explodes. This type of star death is called a supernova.

In the stage of collapse just before the rebound, the heavier elements such as uranium, plutonium, and all of the even heavier elements are created. And in the final explosion, the core of the star, all of the heavy elements from all of its stages of life, are scattered into the Universe as dust.

These dust clouds are later drawn by gravity to other newly forming stars, to become a great swirling disc around them. It is from these dust clouds that planets begin to condense. The remaining hydrogen and helium are also scattered into space, later to join with hydrogen and helium left over from other dying stars, to give birth to a new generation of stars. Thus, the cycle of birth, life, death and rebirth is established even in the stars themselves.

If a star has less than a certain amount of hydrogen, rather than explode the star will continue to collapse inward on itself, to become an even more compact star, called a White Dwarf. The same cycle of fusion continues to take place although in a much more contracted state. Ultimately, the White Dwarf will experience a further stage of collapse, and become a Neutron star, whose matter is so dense that very little energy is able to escape. If our own bodies were collapsed to the density of a Neutron star, we could easily play football on the head of a pin. Were the Earth similarly collapsed, it would fit very easily into a large house, with plenty of room left over for a billiard table!

And yet, this is *still* not the final stage of collapse. In the final stage the Neutron star collapses to become a Black Hole, matter so dense that even light cannot escape from it. Matter has returned to nearly its original density, that of the Universe a few seconds after the Big Bang, but with one major difference – this time the energy, now compressed to matter, is in a much higher state of order.

The vast majority of stars are of the first type, the 'exploding' type. This is because the Universe is still mostly made from hydrogen, so there is still plenty of it around for new stars of the first type to develop. At the least, three-fourths of the Universe is still hydrogen.

So, in the life and death of stars we see another universal pattern – the movement from chaos to order to even higher order. It begins with the disorder of a stellar gas cloud, and moves toward our own level of density with the highest state of order in the emerging Universe: the Mineral Kingdom.

From the Mineral Kingdom are born planets.

And planets, in their own life process, are continually reprocessing the Mineral Kingdom through this same phase of disorder, order, and new order.

Birth, life, death and rebirth.

2

Order

About 5 thousand million years ago, a cloud of remnant hydrogen and dust from perhaps dozens of dead stars began to contract. This contraction was caused by gravitational attraction between different parts of the cloud, perhaps helped along by the solar wind from surrounding stars. As the contraction continued, locally denser areas began to develop.

Stars are born in batches, and somewhere in the Milky Way are the sisters and brothers of our own star, formed from this same cloud complex 5 thousand million years ago. Even among stars, there are family relationships.

So then, within one of these denser gas patches, the collision of atoms began to heat it, and fusion began: the first four hydrogen atoms combined to form a helium, releasing the first photon. Gradually, the photon began to work its way toward the surface, a journey taking perhaps a million years, to at last burst free.

Our Sun had come into life, spreading its new-born light through the dust cloud surrounding it. The dust and gas furthest from the centre of the cloud were, at the same time, coalescing through several stages of the Mineral Kingdom to form planets – among these the Earth.

Atoms moving into new relationships to form minerals; minerals moving into new relationships to form rocks; rocks moving into new relationships to form planets.

Dust grains within the cooling nebulae colliding and fusing to one another, gradually forming larger and larger planetary bodies which themselves collide to form even larger ones. Thus planets are born.

So Earth was born.

All of the planets and moons of the solar system appear to

have formed around the same time by the end of the accumulation stage.

There is considerable evidence for this idea of the formation of the solar system, both from meteorites, and from rocks brought back from the Moon. Meteorites are fragments from the break-up of earlier planetary bodies in the solar system, as is the astroid belt between Mars and Jupiter. There are two major types of meteorites – 'irons', composed mostly of various alloys or iron, and 'stones', composed primarily of minerals such as found in the mantle of the Earth.

There is one other type of stoney meteorite that appears to have never got as far as being part of a planetary body, and gives us a great deal of insight into the original birth of the Mineral Kingdom from stellar dust. This type is rich in carbon, called the carbonaceous chondrites. They have chemical, mineral and textural features which suggest that they are probably remnants left over from the early stages of the newly forming solar system. These chondrites are very close in composition to the non-gaseous make-up of the Sun. Chondrites may have formed even before our own dust cloud condensed to form the solar system, and could be remnants of earlier stages of planetary formation around suns which died to supply the material for our own solar system. There is even evidence that the earliest organic life-forms in the Universe may have begun to evolve in connection with the chondrites. This is discussed in Chapter Three.

As we are now starting to look at the mineral nature of the Universe, I want to pause here and define a few terms. The first term is *mineral:* a mineral is an inorganic substance produced by nature, that has a specific chemical make-up. An example would be the mineral calcite. It is made from calcium, carbon and oxygen, in the ratios 1:1:3. It forms atomic structures based on the rhombahedron, (see Figure 1). There is another chemical substance whose structure is identical, but has manganese in place of calcium in the structure. Because it is a different chemical make-up it becomes a different mineral, called rhodochrosite.

Fig. 1 A rhombahedron

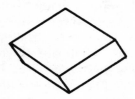

So, with a few exceptions, a different chemical make-up gives us a different mineral name.

The exceptions are when two minerals have the same chemical make-up, but those chemicals are arranged in different structures.

For example, iron and sulphur atoms can be arranged in cubes giving the mineral pyrite, or 'fool's gold.' Or the same atoms can form in rather elongated, shoebox-like structures, in which case the mineral is called marcasite.

A *crystal* occurs when a mineral forms in such a way that flat faces are produced, which are arranged in geometric patterns (cubes, octahedrons, etc.) This usually occurs when there is some sort of opening available in the Earth – usually a crack or fracture (but very seldom in caves, as is commonly believed). Some sort of fluid, usually water at extremely high pressure and temperature, or even molten rock, flows through the open space, depositing on the walls dissolved mineral matter. When the space is not filled in, the forming crystals don't crowd together, and the flat faces characteristic of crystals are not obliterated.

The reason a crystal has flat faces in an outer geometric form is because of the precise patterns its atoms make. *There are only fourteen basic patterns from which all crystals form,* and the outer form is a perfect reflection of the inner form. We can tell exactly how a crystal is arranged inside by looking at the physical forms that appear on the outside. A perfect example of microcosm and macrocosm.

A *rock* is a substance which is made up from two or more

minerals, and makes up a substantial portion of the Earth. An example is the rock granite, made from the minerals quartz, feldspar, and mica. A rock forms when the hollow space described above fills in. The inner, atomic structure remains, but because the forming crystals are all crowded together, the outer form is obliterated. This is called the *crystalline* state. It's a bit like cramming fifteen people into a Volkswagen. The inner structure is still there, but ... Roughly 99 per cent of the Mineral Kingdom is in a crystalline state. But because the inner atomic pattern is preserved, the energy effects are the same in a fragment as in a crystal, because the energy effects of crystals occur at the atomic, and sub-atomic levels.

The most important part of all of this is the fourteen patterns which generate the whole Mineral Kingdom – and as a result, planets, moons, asteroids, meteors, and interstellar dust. In other words, most of the solid universe.

All made from only fourteen basic patterns.

The next time you are in the mountains or in a place where you can see a large area of the mineral Earth, imagine all of it made from only fourteen patterns.

Because these patterns are atomic patterns, and are therefore at a fundamental level also *energy* patterns, these fourteen are the most basic patterns from which the Universe creates itself.

Bear this in mind as we follow the birth of our own Earth and Moon.

Age determinations of moon rocks have shown the Moon to have formed 4.6 thousand million years ago, making it exactly the same age as the Earth, thus it must have been forming at the same time, lending further support to the ideas of solar system formation just described.

Moon rocks are very similar to certain types of Earth rock such as volcanic lavas, which on the Moon are very much like those erupted from Earth volcanoes. The minerals (crystals) discovered on the Moon are pretty much the same as the Earth's. In Moon rocks about forty mineral species have been recognized, with only a very few new, and sub-microscopic minerals being discovered. Since we are discovering several new minerals each year on the Earth as well, there is no particular implication to the discovery of different minerals in minute amounts elsewhere in the solar system. Remember too, there are very few Earth rocks that have had the same high degree of scrutiny as Moon rocks.

In the early stages the Moon went through a number of geological processes in its development that were identical to Earth processes. Because the Moon is a smaller body and therefore of a considerably different overall composition, certain geological processes which continue to shape and reshape the Earth today died out within about a thousand million years of the formation of the Moon.

Moonquakes still occur though, showing us that although the Moon 'lives' more slowly than the Earth, it is by no means lifeless. Our studies of the moon show us one thing for certain. It is part of the brotherhood and sisterhood of planetary bodies that formed simultaneously – the family called 'the solar system'.

Returning to the Earth now, let us focus on its formation and the processes which shaped and continue to reshape the Earth, keeping it a vital, living planet.

As the Earth grew in size from the accumulating debris of the solar nebulae, its interior was heated by the decay of radioactive atoms. The long-lived varieties of uranium, thorium, and potassium continue to be an important heat source from within the earth today. This internal heating produced melting and remelting allowing the metallic iron compounds, being heavier than other newly forming minerals, to sink towards the centre of the Earth to form the core. The silicates formed the outer shell, or mantle, of the Earth (see Figure 2). As the heating continued some melting of the mantle occurred and the lighter mineral portion rose to the surface to form the crust. As this occurred, water was released from some of these recrystallized minerals to form the primitive oceans. Also during this early stage, large scale convection currents were established in the semi-solid mantle. These cur-

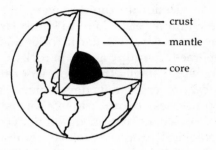

Fig. 2 Section of the Earth

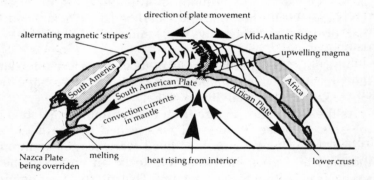

Fig. 3

rents carry heat from the interior to the surface and aid in the separation of lighter and denser minerals (see Figure 3). These currents are important in many of the geological processes occurring at the surface of the Earth and provide the energies for the movement for the continents, leading ultimately to the surface of the Earth 'recycling' itself.

We learned about how the Earth is structured by studying

the speed of earthquake waves through various representative types of rock. We have established a relationship between rock density and the speed that various waves travel. We can then measure the movement of the same type of waves through the Earth, and observe the variations of density within the Earth.

There are two major zones easily observable through the measurement of earthquake waves in the outermost portion of the Earth, the crust. Two distinct types of crust are found: oceanic and continental. The crust beneath the oceans, which comprises about 70 per cent of the surface of the Earth, is of a fairly uniform thickness of about 3 miles (4.8 kilometres) and is composed of rocks made up primarily of melted mantle material. *All* of the present ocean crust has been created within the last 200 million years.

The crust under the continents is more complicated and has a more variable thickness and a less defined structure. In areas that have not undergone mountain building, continental crust has an average thickness of about 22 miles (35.4 kilometres), while under mountain belts it can be as thick as 30 miles (48.3 kilometres). Even so, if the Earth were the size of a football (a soccer ball), the thickest crust would be no thicker than a postage stamp.

We have detailed studies of the upper part of the crust, as drill holes have penetrated to a depth of five miles or so. It is covered with a thin layer of sediments, and is mostly composed of a granite-like rock called granodiorite, whose most common minerals are felspar, quartz, hornblende, and pyroxene.

We believe that the crust which forms the continents is produced uniformly with time, and that the area of the continents is still growing at the present day. Continental crust is probably produced by remelting of the oceanic crust. The crust makes up less than 1 per cent of the Earth by volume, and less than 0.5 per cent by mass. The majority of crystals you will encounter are generated in the crust, and are generally of lighter minerals. These are minerals such as quartz (in its varieties as rock crystal, agate, amethyst, citrine, etc.), and topaz, tourmaline, ruby, sapphire, turquoise, etc.

The mantle makes up approximately 83 per cent of the Earth by volume, and 67 per cent by mass. The minerals that make up the mantle are mainly magnesium-iron silicates.

The composition of stoney meteorites, which make up 93 per cent of all types of meteorites, has strongly influenced our thinking on the composition of the mantle. It is believed that these types of meteorites show us a great deal about the early composition of the solar system, and their mineralogy is consistent with what we know of the mantle from other sources.

The core of the Earth extends from the base of the mantle to the centre of the Earth, and contains 16 per cent of the volume and 32 per cent of the mass of the Earth.

The core is metallic, and consists of two parts. The outer core does not transmit certain types of earthquake waves, and must be liquid; the inner core is solid and is thought to be composed of an iron-nickel alloy similar to that found in meteorites, as its measured density is the same as that of nickel-iron meteorites. We can easily compute the density of the mantle and crust. When combined with the calculated density for a core of nickel iron, we get a correct average density for the Earth as a whole – the core must be close to the make-up of those types of meteorites.

It is thought that with the outer core being liquid and the inner core being solid, slippage occurs between the inner core and the mantle, with the outer core acting as a 'lubricant', generating the magnetic field of the Earth.

One thing that is absolutely certain is that the Earth is not hollow, as suggested by several recent writers. The worldwide system set up for the monitoring of earthquakes, and more recently in both Eastern and Western countries for watching each other's underground nuclear tests, would spot such a thing instantly.

One of the most exciting discoveries about the Earth has taken place in the twenty years or so since I was studying geology in university. At the time, the idea that the continents moved about across the surface of the Earth was only believed by wild-eyed radicals and long-haired hippies. The idea has been around for a hundred years or so, but it was only with the further development of our ability to measure, in this case the rocks of the ocean floors, that we began to see this was actually what was happening. And from this ability to measure, called science, we began to see the mechanisms by which the Earth could be said to be 'alive' – an aliveness the mystics have always known about.

One of the first major discoveries was that the magnetic field on the ocean bottoms was arranged in stripes, running parallel to the crests of ocean ridges, and this pattern usually extended all the way from the ridge to the flanking continents. It was noticed that the stripes were not only parallel to the ridge crests, but they also had identical patterns on either side of the ridge, and that any variation in the patterns on one side of the ridge could be matched on the other (see Figure 3). It was also noticed that the widths of successive strips exactly matched in proportion the known time periods of normal and reversed polarity of the Earth's magnetic field.

By the way, reversal of the Earth's magnetic field does *not* mean that the Earth physically tipped upside down, as is often interpreted by writers such as Velikovsky. It simply means that the *magnetism* of the Earth reversed itself. Why it does so isn't certain.

If the Earth had 'tipped over' in the past, and it is suggested that this has taken place as late as 800 BC, then why are the astronomical alignments at Stonehenge, and literally hundreds of other standing stone alignments, still perfect. Even the *slightest* movement of the Earth would have destroyed the alignments.

In observing the stripes on the ocean floor, the suggestion was put forth that the ocean floor was behaving like the tape in an enormous tape recorder. It was recording the changes in the polarity in the Earth's magnetic field as the continents moved apart, and molten material from the Earth's interior welled up to occupy the gap between. Rocks have no magnetic properties while they are hot, but as they cool they can become weak permanent magnets 'freezing' into their mineral structure some 'memory' of the magnetic field in which they are cooled.

Eventually it was discovered by submarine photography that this is exactly what was happening – ˙ new material (lavas) can be observed welling up along these ridges today – and this will cool with the magnetic properties related to the Earth's present magnetic field. It has now been discovered that there is a fairly consistent rate of spreading and movement of the continents on a worldwide basis, varying at a rate from 0.8 to 5.5 inches (2 – 14 centimetres) per year.

It was also realized that the creation of new ocean floor in the centres of the oceans meant that the old ocean floor had to be disappearing somewhere else, in order to accommodate the new surface area. It was known that there were very deep valleys, called trenches, found in many oceans, which were particularly well developed around the western and northern sides of the Pacific Ocean. These trenches are elongated furrows in the ocean floor and in them water depths range between 5.5 and 6.8 miles (9 – 11 kilometres), roughly twice the average depth of the oceans. And, on the side of the trench towards the nearest continent, there is everywhere a parallel ridge, which from place to place breaks the surface to give small islands that are volcanic in origin, although some now carry a capping of recent coral. Almost all of the present volcanic activity of the western Pacific Ocean lies along such ridges, immediately west of the deep trenches.

In these trenches, the ocean floor which had been created much earlier at a ridge, turns downward and is pulled back into the mantle. As it is pulled under it remelts. Because it is crustal material and therefore lighter than the mantle, the molten material begins to work its way back upward, although at a distance from where it was originally pulled under. This is the material that re-erupts as lava, forming the parallel chain of volcanoes (see Figure 4).

A Plate is a single unit of crust, which moves as a single piece. The Earth's plates, and their directions of movement are shown in Figure 5.

Fig. 4 Volcanoes along a plate margin

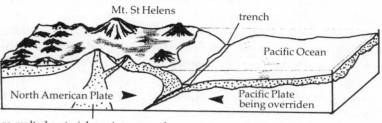

Fig. 5 Major plates of the Earth and their direction of movement

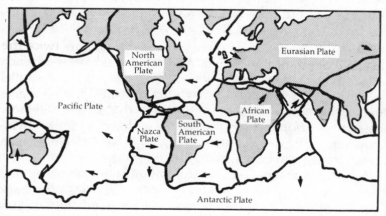

Another plate where remelting is taking place is along the Pacific Coast of the USA, where the Pacific Plate is being over-ridden by the North American Plate. As the material from the Pacific Plate is remelted, it re-emerges as a chain of volcanoes along the margin of North America. Mount St Helens, Mt

Shasta, and Mt Hood are examples.

A similar process created Mt Etna and Mt Vesuvius in Europe, where the Eurasian Plate is overriding the African Plate.

It was once proposed to dispose of the Earth's rubbish by tipping it into the ocean trenches, but some wit then pointed out that in a few years the nearby volcanoes would be "spitting out old refrigerators".

This process of continual movement, melting, crystallization, remelting and recrystallization is a characteristic of the life process of our planet. Through this process, the earth constantly (albeit slowly related to a human lifetime), renews itself.

Your own body also undergoes continual change. If you are over thirty, you don't have the same body you were born with. Your skin renews itself every seven years, for example. Other cells in other organs take a greater or lesser amount of time, but by the age of thirty, there are very few cells left that are 'originals'.

So now we've seen about the *how*. Now let's look at the *why*: the consciousness behind it all.

As forms began to get more complex, from gas to solid, solid to mineral, mineral to planet, so the underlying consciousness began to develop greater complexity, and greater capacity for experience. The development of higher awareness, and even life itself seems to be related to the complexities of form.

Robert Prinable of Self Transformation Seminars has noted that: "Structure is form, and life is the flow of energy through form." The more complex the form, the greater the number of choices of ways in which energy can flow. When we build this principle into a machine, we call it a computer. When we develop it in the Animal Kingdom, we call it the brain.

The first structures through which energy flowed, the minerals, were far removed from the vast complexity of the brain however. Remember that we are still dealing at the mineral level with only fourteen fundamental patterns. In the mineral world we can build a couple of hundred combinations of forms from these, whereas the biological Kingdoms have over half a million compounds of carbon alone.

But for the minerals, it is enough.

The overriding fields of consciousness that evolved for the lower Kingdoms are often referred to as *Devas*, or nature spirits, or elementals, or even angels. I happen to prefer the word Deva, although all of the others mean essentially the same thing. The word itself comes from Sanskrit, and means 'a being of light'. But none of them really describes what it *is*. The Deva (or any of the other names) is basically a field of consciousness, which has as its purpose to bring itself into manifestation in the lowest possible levels of energy; for us, the physical plane. Thus, all that has form has a consciousness behind it. A Deva is composite being, being made up of a number of different levels of consciousness, each level of consciousness having a correspondence to some aspect of the natural world. As an example, the Plant Kingdom will have an overseeing Deva, that might be called the Plant Deva, and making up the total consciousness of this greater Deva, would be lesser devas of trees or flowers, and they in turn are made up of even smaller units, such as Deva of Oak trees or the Deva of Spruce trees. Although these 'Lower Devas' are often perceived as separate entities, they are in reality just aspects of the greater entity, The Plant Deva.

Even further, there are two types of Devas, those of the natural realms, and those which are created by human thought. We human beings vastly underestimate the power of our own thoughts, and if enough people believe or think a certain thing, a self-sustaining thought-form is created, which essentially becomes an overriding consciousness, ultimately having the power to perpetuate itself. Examples of Devas created by human thought are the Devas of particular cities, which take on the collective consciousness of all of those who dwell in them or Devas of a particular occupation or profession, especially those which require a great deal of human thought and activity, or even the Deva of a particular sport. You can demonstrate this to yourself – attend a sporting event sometime of a sport in which you have no particular interest, and be sensitive to the 'atmosphere' that builds as the game progresses. This energy field is the thought-form being built by the collective consciousness of all those present. Another example of such a form being created is the entity which turns a group of human beings into a mob, often encouraging individuals in that mob to perform actions that would normally be abhorrent to them.

As it turns out, science has already studied this. Of course, scientists use different terms, but later as we look at the biological Kingdoms in Chapter Three, especially the parts about animal behaviour, think back to this and see if it isn't the same thing.

Obviously some of these thought-forms are shortlived, depending on the activity involved, but many of them pass on to become part of the collective consciousness; thus a relatively small number of people acting in concert can begin to influence all of humanity. So it is that the 'Aquarian Age' will begin, literally, to 'take form'. Even a numerically small number of enlightened people can have an effect out of proportion to their numbers.

The term Crystal Deva which I often use is my own personal term. The name Deva of the Mineral Kingdom would be equally applicable, although the fundamental unit of the Mineral Kingdom is the Crystal, and all structures of the Mineral Kingdom (rocks and planets) are built from crystals, or in some cases molten crystals (as in water, the molten form of the mineral ice).

As in the other Kingdoms, the Mineral Kingdom also has its Lesser Devas ranging from the individual Devas of various rocks and minerals, to the overseeing presence that I have termed the Crystal Deva.

As the solid portion of the Universe is made from crystals, the Crystal Deva is part of a universal field of consciousness that we often refer to as 'God'.

From early Deva contacts, I learned a great deal about the nature of Devas. First and foremost, Devas only have interest in that which they are the Deva of. For example, the Tree Deva is no particularly interested in flowers or shrubs, except as they relate to its propagation of trees. Likewise, the Deva of water-lilies has no particular interest in the Deva of mudlarks, except as they relate to the survival of the water-lily. The Deva's function is to create in the physical realm that which it is the Deva of, at every possible opportunity.

This is equally true in the Mineral Kingdom. For example, quartz crystals, as well as most other vein-growing crystals, will grow at odd angles in a vein in order to fill the largest space available, thus growing the largest crystal possible. This adjustment of the growing direction of crystals to fill the available space would be a function of the Deva of Quartz Crystals.

In the beginning my first perception of the Crystal Deva was as an entity separate from myself. The really conscious contacts began at the time I was writing my book *Cosmic Crystals,* when I found that there appeared to be gaps in my own knowledge, from both the scientific and the mystical point of view. Knowing I had the ability to contact Devas (as I would have expressed it at that time) I set out to contact the Deva in the same way in which I would have attempted to contact Spirit Guides or any other discarnate entity.

This process is related to astral projection, nothing more than just being aware of the part of your Self that exists outside the physical body, in this case coexisting with the Mineral Kingdom. As I later became aware, each and every human being has an indwelling presence of the Crystal Deva as part of the physical body. This is related principally to the lower two chakras and is directly connected to the mineral aspect of the human body. Your body, if broken down into component parts, would be about enough water to fill half a bath tub, and about three cups of dry powder – all minerals (as previously mentioned, water is the molten form of the mineral ice).

At any rate, in the first contact the Deva was seen as an external being, and the contact consisted on my part of questions and answers to various aspects of the Mineral Kingdom, and especially about the structure and movement of energy in crystals. The answers and explanations were quite precise and technical, resulting in a deeper understanding of the mechanisms of crystal energy, which led me to search in different areas of the scientific literature that I had not previously thought of exploring. And lo and behold, I began to discover that scientific research had advanced further than I had realized into the movement of energy in crystal structures, and corresponded exactly with what I had been told by the Deva.

I believe that it is vitally important in any sort of 'spirit' contact to check out and verify factually as much information as possible at all times. This is the only way you can be sure of the accuracy of your source, which ultimately is the inner You, as there is a general and often quite wrong assumption that anything coming from a 'spirit' source is accurate. In many cases this is simply not so, and depends on the level of the 'source' itself, which in the final reality is the projection of the inner source of the 'medium'. What you 'channel' is therefore an exact replica of your own inner state. There are depths to each of us that are often unplumbed consciously, and this is why a medium will often look at something he or she has 'channelled', and say something like: "That couldn't possibly have come from *me*."

Outside of the investigations through the Deva for my own personal information, the first actual 'channelling' took place in 1983.

I began by letting my consciousness sink into my own physical body, and became aware as I did so of a growing presence which seemed to surround me. The Devic presence surrounds us anyway but because it is part of our own nature we seldom focus on it, or for that matter even notice it.

From my own earlier experience with the Deva, I had warned the group to ask very precise questions, as precision is the key note of the Mineral Kingdom. The Deva would therefore answer exactly the question that was asked, although the person asking the question may have had a different intention in mind. This had the effect of requiring the questioner to examine very carefully in his or her own mind exactly what they wished to ask. It was also important not to ask questions that could be answered with a simple yes or no, as no matter how long and convoluted the question was, the reply would simply be one word or the other. The requirement to ask precise questions was a benefit to everyone in the group as the answers that came back reflected the clarity of questioning. This sort of 'reflection' back to the questioner was the basis for my realization of how crystals really work in relation to the Human Kingdom (see Chaper Six).

The reason for such answers is not that the Deva is trying to be difficult but that at the mineral level of consciousness, there is virtually no free will, and therefore the Deva cannot interpret questions, but can only answer exactly what is asked. Secondly, the answers can only reflect from the point of view of the Mineral Kingdom. The Deva made it quite clear in some of the early questioning that it could not answer from the point of view of the Plant Kingdom, the Animal Kingdom, or the Human Kingdom, as such levels of consciousness were energetically above itself, and were therefore inaccessible to it.

The Crystal Deva is a major part of the Earth Deva. The Earth is still 99.9 per cent minerals, and minerals supply the building blocks for the other Kingdoms. In contacts with the Earth Deva, answers were therefore very much from the point of view of the Earth's Mineral nature.

Another interesting aspect of the direct contact was the voice of the Deva, which was quite flat and expressionless. Although not a monotone, the voice was nonetheless totally devoid of any human quality. This is, of course, because the Deva is *not* human and therefore all human qualities of emotion, compassion, love, and so forth, do not exist at that level of consciousness. Many people found it to be quite an unsettling experience to be presented with a voice speaking from a point of Universal awareness, and yet devoid of these qualities. A further reflection indeed on the higher nature of the human being.

Also in this contact, everyone in the room was experiencing distinct physical reactions. I felt as if I was being crushed into the floor and weighed ten times my normal weight. Others in the room reported similar sensations, and in following courses where the Deva was channelled, 80-90 per cent had similar experiences of immense density. In later workshops I would often ask people to attempt to lift their arm out of their lap or from the arm of the chair during this experience of density, and many people found themselves unable to do so.

Although we were seeing the Deva as a separate entity at that time, what we were really focussing on was our own mineral nature, and its own experience of density.

Another common experience was totally forgetting the questions we wished to ask. The density was so great, many felt their minds totally incapable of functioning. In later workshops, I asked people to write their questions down beforehand so that they could remember them when the time came.

It became apparent that this experience of extreme density was the experience of a soul in its first incarnation on the Earth. Remembering my own experience of this, it was nearly identical – the feeling of being weighed down, and of the immense effort necessary just to move my body from place to place, much less do anything creative with it. It is the sort of experience many of us reproduce on Monday morning.

So why all this emphasis on density?

The movement into density is the most fundamental activity of the Universe. I'll say that one again.

The movement into density is the most fundamental activity of the Universe.

Think about it.

The Universe is still almost all made from hydrogen.

Look up in the sky tonight. What do you see?

Stars.

Thousands of stars, and beyond them hundreds of thousands of millions of millions of stars.

Doing one thing.

Taking hydrogen, and making heavy stuff out of it.

The Universe is getting denser.

And the first thing it does with newly minted heavy stuff is make crystals out of it.

Are you getting the idea about why they are important?

Crystals are fundamental structures of Creation. They are also the very first stage in making heavy matter into *you.*

It takes a while.

It has taken the Universe 15 *thousand million* years to make you.

You are the *end product* of 15 thousand million years of Universal evolution.

In order to make you, the Universe had had to invent galaxies. And stars. And planets. And DNA. And bacteria. And animals. Just to make *you.*

Seems a helluva lot of bother, doesn't it?

Seen from this perspective, could you doubt that there is a *purpose* to your being? And that there is some sort of basic connection between you and the Mineral Kingdom?

I'm often asked about the relationships between various parts of the Universe. The Deva once gave by far the best answer I have ever heard: "Stars are the womb of my creation – planets are the fruit of my loins, and the interstellar dust and gas clouds are my seed."

The mineral Kingdom is constantly renewing and re-forming itself, mostly through the processes that activate continental drift. Crystal material is remelted in ocean trenches, and there is a continual up and down movement of the continental masses. Broad downwarps, called geosynclines, fill with sometimes thousands of feet of sediments. As heat increases with depth, sediments melt or fuse, forming different minerals from the old materials.

In this way the Mineral Kingdom experiences itself through changing forms. In the quartz crystal you hold in your hand, some of the silicon atoms may once have been part of a feldspar crystal, others from a garnet. The oxygens may have come from a calcite, or hematite.

Are minerals evolving then? Not in the sense of biological evolution, where new patterns are created. The laws of physics lock the Mineral Kingdom into its basic forms. It can experience itself through all of its possible forms though, by the processes just described. The study of those processes of mineral life is called Geology.

There is one other important way that the Mineral Kingdom gains experience that perhaps you haven't thought of – through contact with *you*.

See you in Chapter Six for that one.

3

Ooze

As we have seen in the last chapter, the development of the Mineral Kingdom, although the first step toward advancing consciousness in the Universe, was still largely governed by a relatively narrow band of laws, relating to the chemistry and physics of the crystalline state. There were no choices involved, because at any particular state of temperature and pressure, there is only one possible mineral combination that can take place. The relationships that govern the formation of minerals are purely electronic, and the 'attractiveness' of one set of atoms for another is extremely limited.

When organic life began to appear in the Universe, the explosion of choice was as dramatic as the Big Bang itself. But if there had been anyone around to see it, it would have gone almost unnoticed, because the life-forms themselves were too small to see. And yet from these minute beginnings, the energetic foundations of the Universe were rocked, and the transformation of the Universe began that is still going on today. It is part of who *you* are.

Exactly how organic life originated is not known, but we do know certain things about it, and suspect other things very strongly. The eminent astronomer Fred Hoyle makes a very strong case for life not originating on the Earth, but rather suggests that organic life is scattered throughout the Universe, and in fact may exist nearly everywhere in simple forms.

The biology of life-forms is likely to have certain similarities everywhere in the Universe – the chemical reactions related to these life-forms are all designed around the basic chemistry of the carbon atom. As carbon is one of the major products of stellar evolution, it is one of the most common elements of the

Universe, and as it is virtually the only common element with the chemistry necessary to develop the complex combinations necessary for biological life, it is likely that most major life-forms in the Universe will be, in some manner or another, carbon based. For example, sugars are one of the main energy sources of life – and these are built up of the two commonest molecules in the Universe: the molecules of hydrogen and carbon monoxide. Thus the enzymes we use to unlock the energy content of the sugars are engaged in processes which are central to the chemical content of the whole Universe. Therefore there are not vast numbers of equally likely systems to produce organic life – it is even doubtful there is as much as *one* other system.

The idea that life has evolved on the Earth spontaneously revolves around some experiments done earlier in the century. If you mix up simple molecules like water, ammonia, methane, carbon dioxide and hydrogen cyanide with almost any type of intense energy, such as ultra-violet light or electricity, some of the molecules reassemble themselves into amino acids, which are the individual building blocks of proteins. But, no one has shown that the correct arrangements of amino acids, such as the orderings and the enzymes, can be produced by this method. This is a huge jump in complexity, and it is highly unlikely, according to Hoyle, that such a jump could have taken place in the time allotted to it in the early development of life-forms on the Earth. Hoyle describes its likelihood by giving a comparable example:

> "A junk yard contains all the bits and pieces of a Boeing 747, dismembered and in disarray. A whirlwind happens to blow through the yard. What is the chance that after its passage the fully assembled 747, ready to fly, will be found standing there? So small as to be negligible, even if a tornado were to blow through enough junk yards to fill the whole Universe."[2]

So, if life did not originate on the Earth, then where did it originate, and how did it get here?

It seems likely that organic life originated in a number of places in the Universe at the same time, remembering that in the early days of the Universe everything was much closer together, which increased the likelihood of interchanges between stars and galaxies, and there was a great deal more free debris moving about in intergalactic space to act as 'messengers' to carry life. There is even evidence as to how this came about.

A Dutch scientist, Hans Phlug, detected the remains of life from outside the Earth in a meteorite, one of the formerly described carbonaceous chondrites. Within this meteorite are preserved the remains of once living organisms. These microorganisms have similarities to a terrestrial bacterium, *pedomicrobium* (see Figure 6).

Fig. 6 A pedomicrobium

As well as finding evidence of bacteria in the meteorite, Phlug also found other structures very similar to Earth viruses. These formerly living remains came from one meteorite, one which fell over a hundred years ago.

Also discovered in these meteorites were amino acids, which can be chemically similar but structurally distinct. These could be thought of as 'left hand' or 'right hand'. There are many amino acids which exist in these forms, but living organisms predominantly use left-handed forms, the types that turned up in the meteorite, giving even further evidence that these are the remains of living organisms.

What I find so intriguing about the discovery of a pedomicrobium type of bacterium, is that it 'feeds' on metal compounds. Its main biochemical processes consist of transferring oxygen from some salt either to ferrous iron or manganese, which releases energy for the bacterium. As a waste product, a metallic oxide is produced, which is transferred to the 'root', where it accumulates. What this implies, is that to develop and survive this type of bacteria does not need the complex combination that the Earth produces – plenty of free water, masses of free oxygen in the atmosphere, and moderate temperature and pressure changes. It can survive and thrive under what to Earth life would be remarkably harsh and hostile – and instantly fatal – conditions.

We could easily envisage the evolution of other primitive life-forms on a planet or planetoid in the early Universe: a great deal of free carbon, perhaps more surface electrical activity, much less free oxygen and considerable carbon dioxide in the atmosphere. On such a planet the complex interchanges needed to develop the long-chain carbon molecules which are the building blocks of organic life, would have had opportunities to develop at a very early stage of the Universe.

As the Universe is approximately 15 thousand million years old, and we know of organic life on Earth for only about a fifth of that time, it seems highly likely that primitive organic life originated much earlier on in the newly formed Universe, perhaps beginning as little as a thousand million years into the infant Universe.

This original life was probably viruses, which can develop under immensely hostile conditions. They have a tremendous capacity to survive extremes of heat and cold, and the extremely high amounts of radioactivity which would have dominated the early forming Universe. Because viruses can attach to, and alter one another, relatively short and simple chains probably evolved first, perhaps large numbers of them simultaneously, linking and altering each other to produce more viable forms.

Much more complex forms, such as bacteria, are found in

the water at the core of nuclear reactors, suggesting that the much simpler viruses would have a higher toleration for radiation.

Viruses have the ability to alter one another, combining to form longer chains of molecules, which ultimately evolve into bacteria. Bacteria are much more complex and thus are more vulnerable, and yet we see that bacteria can survive very hostile conditions.

A medical researcher, Lewis Thomas, recently said of viruses:

"The viruses, instead of being single-minded agents of disease and death, now begin to look more like mobile genes. We live in a dancing matrix of viruses; they dart, rather like bees, from organism to organism, from plant to insect to mammal to me and back again, and into the sea tugging along pieces of this genome, strings of genes from that, transplanting grafts of DNA passing around heredity as though at a great party. They may be mechanisms for keeping new DNA in the widest circulation among us."[3]

So, viruses look a good bet to be the original life-forms. We have tended to view viruses as the 'bad actors' on the stage of Life. *They may, in fact be the Universe's fundamental organic life-form.*

So, how did life spread through the Universe? One answer is through comets and other planetary debris, which tend to move through inter-planetary space. Even today in a much expanded Universe, there still appears to be overlapping between our own solar system and nearby stars by cometary bodies.

But is it possible for organic life to survive the incredibly harsh environment of space? The principle hazard to micro-organisms in space is the destructive effect of X-rays.

This radiation can damage the genetic equipment of a cell, even killing it. But many micro-organisms are known to possess an amazingly efficient repair process. In one experiment, bacteria were exposed to enormous amounts of X-rays –

enough to kill a human, and which made more than ten thousand breakages in its genetic material. And yet the bacteria proceeded to repair this horrendous damage, and became viable once again.

In another example, the Surveyor III space craft which landed on the Moon in 1967 inadvertantly carried living bacteria, which were retrieved two years later by the crew of Apollo XIII – they were still thriving.

From there, it is a short step to see that if micro-organisms do exist in space, and in the quantity that there appears to be evidence of, *the Earth with its 'organic soup' oceans would have been a fertile breeding ground for the hearty life-forms seeded on to Earth from the surrounding cosmos.* And although the conditions on the early and newly formed Earth would have been hostile to most present life-forms, it would have been a veritable 'Garden of Eden' to life-forms that perhaps evolved in, and survived the trip across, interstellar space.

But what happened once they got here?

A struggle to survive and multiply?

Probably not.

Most likely there was a series of genetic interchanges between seeded viruses and newly emerging bacteria, generating new species, and modifying old ones. This even appears to be going on today, as suspicion is growing that 'flu' viruses may well be coming from space.

Thomas notes:

> "Most of the associations between living things we know about are essentially cooperative ones ...; when they have the look of adversaries, it is usually a stand-off relation, with one party ... flagging the other off.
>
> Even when circumstances require that there be winners and losers, the transaction is not necessarily a combat."[4]

We are now beginning to understand what appears to be the nature of most living things: to pool resources, and to fuse when possible.

Thomas suggests that:

"The urge of almost all animals to make rhythmic sounds may be a restatement of an early memory, perhaps going back even to this time – the 'score for the transformation of inanimate, random matter in chaos into the improbable, ordered dance of living forms. Morowitz has presented the case ... that a steady flow of energy from ... sun to the ... earth is mathematically destined to cause the organization of matter into an increasingly ordered state."[5]

Is this, then, the underlying mechanism propelling the first primitive life-forms through time to become YOU?

And all other living things on the Earth.

It looks like it.

How did it come about?

There is a natural inclination in unrelated cells to combine to form hybrid cells. Immune systems evolved specifically to prevent this from happening. Without this mechanism, there would be no individual creatures, no plants, no animals. Only a continuous organic skin over the whole Earth. In your own body, the immune systems revolve around the lymphocytes, a type of white blood cell, programmed by their genetics to be explorers; to wander through the body, asking all other cells encountered only one question: Are you the same molecular shape as me? If not, all hell breaks loose, as we'll see later.

There are so many of them, that collectively they can search out anything foreign, no matter what its source. Some of them are even equipped to fight substances that don't even exist until they are invented in a laboratory. So, not only are they programmed collectively to recognize a natural threat to the genetic programme of their host, but also to make a very good guess.

The lymphocytes originally evolved as separate creatures in the 'soup', and attached themselves to other evolving cells in a symbiotic relationship. A sort of primitive "You scratch my back, I'll scratch yours." Or more like, "You feed me, and I'll guard your genes."

In just this sort of manner, cells began to specialize. In your own body, at a certain stage of your embryo, any cell could become anything. But beyond a certain point, cells make a 'choice' to become heart cells, or bone cells, or elbow cells, etc – they are committed to 'specialize'. You can find all of this in biology books.

Your own body carries in its own development, the history of life on the Earth, which we will look at later on in this chapter.

After the first viruses and then more complex bacteria developed, the next major leap was the release of free oxygen into the water, and later into the atmosphere.

The release of oxygen had to wait for the development of specialized cells capable of photosynthesis. They had to live in an environment with enough sunlight for photosynthesis, but they also needed to be shielded from fatal doses of ultra-violet light. (The stuff that gives you sunburn.) The primitive atmosphere may have done this to some extent, but it is also likely that they developed at some depth under the water, where there was the right balance between light and shielding.

Currents in the water would quickly upset this delicate balance, so it is possible that organic life didn't develop in the oceans, but in lagoons or shallow, undisturbed pools or lakes. But once established, it took over the oceans like wildfire.

Blue green algae, the originators of photosynthesis, merged in a co-operative venture with primitive bacteria cells, and became the chloroplasts (the photosynthesis factories) of the Plant Kingdom.

The first evidence of free oxygen in the atmosphere, rocks containing an oxide of iron, rust, which can only be produced with free oxygen, occurs about 3 thousand million years ago, so the 'seeding' of the Earth would have been much earlier – perhaps even as the primitive Earth was still cooling.

There must have been a slow building of atmospheric oxygen, with many, many species of algae dying out as the atmosphere became more and more processed.

The oxygen you are breathing this moment is the gift of these algae, over 2 thousand million years ago.

The atmosphere of the primitive Earth would have been highly poisonous to any life-forms today – methane, ammonia, carbon monoxide, and nitrogen. The oceans covering most of the planet's surface would have been constantly stirred by volcanic activity and vast electrical storms. The earliest life-forms would have begun to process these various compounds through their own life processes, and release free oxygen as a by-product.

There are still a few of these earliest types of organisms about today on the Earth. They are certain types of viruses, such as those that produce botulism, and types of bacteria that are often found in hot springs – springs which are more like pools of mild sulphuric acid. There are the little bacteria swimming around in this acid, loving every minute of it!

So then, the first stage of evolution on the Earth was to produce the stage setting for the next act: without free oxygen, more complex forms could never have evolved.

Out of all this emerges a picture of the early evolution of both the Plant and Animal Kingdoms – oceans teeming with bacteria, modifying one another, interacting, merging, joining forces to create new and more complex creatures. One of these little creatures paddling about in the early oceans was the germ of the idea that became *you*. The ancestor of your own body was *one individual* in all these billions. In common, of course, with everyone else on the Earth.

Free oxygen was not only necessary for more complex life-forms to develop, but atmospheric oxygen is also our shield against harmful solar radiation, filtering out the exact wavelengths that are dangerous to life. Most likely, it even governed the development of life-forms – those forms vulnerable to the wavelengths it doesn't filter out, which either never developed, or died out as the oxygen content of the atmosphere increased.

As the oxygen content of the seas increased, the earliest bacterial life-forms began to die out. They evolved in an oxygen-deficient environment, so increased oxygen levels were poisonous to them.

More advanced, more complex organisms were well under way by about 570 million years ago, by which time the Animal Kingdom had separated from the Plant Kingdom, and had begun its own evolutionary path. Exactly when this separation took place is unknown, but the earliest evidence that we have of these organisms comes from the Flinders Range in Australia, where fossils approximately 650 million years old have been found. Their preservation was highly unusual. The earliest animals were related to slugs, snails, and jellyfish, all living in the oceans. At that time part of the Flinders Range was a wide sandy beach, and some of these jellyfish-like organisms washed up on the beach, dried in the sun, and were later covered over with sand. Had these animals fallen back into the ocean depths, they would never have been preserved. Until this discovery, the only real evidence that we had of animal life during this period was the borings of worm-like animals preserved in rocks which were once the muds of ocean bottoms, and a few fossil algae.

The real leap into greater complexity came 570 million years ago, when animals with skeletons began to appear for the first time. Like modern insects, these marine animals wore their skeletons on the outside and were called Trilobites (see Figure 7). Shellfish were also evolving by this time.

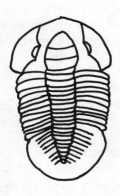

Fig. 7 A trilobite

The next major development began with the evolution of animals who wore their skeletons on the *inside* – fish – which took place around 480 million years ago. This was a major turning point in the development of the Animal Kingdom, for all animals with backbones, including you, evolved from them. And with this new development in structure and complexity, new sorts of possibilities began to open up in the physical body, especially that of mobility. But before this potential could be fully realized, another development had to take place.

Until around 430 million years ago, all organic life was confined to the oceans. Around that time, the first plant life began to move out on to the land. It is important to realize that for nine tenths of the age of the Earth, there was no life whatever on land – life on land is relatively new. And until plant life developed on land, there was no animal life on land, mostly because there was nothing for them to eat!

Meanwhile in the oceans the fishes continued to evolve and develop, and in particular, one fish with rather short, stubby fins, who was probably a Libran (like me), and slightly lazy. This particular fish discovered that he could shuffle along the bottom of the ocean on his fins, and did not have to go to all the work of swimming. Now, Librans may be a bit lazy, but we are also immensely curious, and one day this fish popped up to take a breath (fish had lungs in those days rather than gills), and saw something on a bit of land that looked interesting. Because he had learned to shuffle along on his fins, he was able to move up out of the water for a short distance, and lo and behold, food. Because we Librans also like our vittles, this particular fish became a regular visitor to the land. Soon his friends started noticing that he was on to a good thing and soon enough the word got out. Rather than have to fight and squabble for the food that was available in their particular part of the ocean, many of them soon began to make regular pilgrimages to the land where there was plenty of food to go round. So, by about 400 million years ago, those fishes who had been taking to the land began to evolve their fins into feet (the bone structures of your own feet and hands can be directly traced to the bone structures in the fins of those early fish) and so the first amphibians developed.

The next stage in the development of the physical body that you now wear, began somewhere around 300 million years ago.

This was the evolution of the reptiles, the first animals capable of living entirely on the land. The reptiles occupied a face of the Earth much different from that which we see today. At that time the land surface of the Earth was all joined together in one super continent, call Pangaea. It was on Pangaea that the dinosaurs began to evolve, and by around 200 million years ago, they completely dominated the animal life on the land. This domination was to go on for the next 135 *million years*. The dinosaurs were immensely successful – we as the human race have about 129 million years to go to catch up with them.

Yet they vanished.

Why?

A recent television series looked at the question of dinosaurs and their extinction, which was all very interesting in itself, but for me the most interesting part was a projection at the end of the programme as to what would have happened to the dinosaurs had they continued to evolve. The conclusion was that certain dinosaurs would have ultimately evolved into an upright standing, humanoid-appearing form, as equally capable of higher intelligence and awareness as man. So why did they disappear?

I believe the answer lies in the nature of the reptile body itself. One of the most important differences between reptiles and mammals (us) is that reptiles are unable to regulate their own body temperatures, and if it gets too hot, or too cold, they just die. Clearly on a planet that experiences a great deal of seasonal climatic change, such a body has major limitations. It worked well enough for the dinosaurs while Pangaea mostly occupied a position on the Earth in more or less tropical zones, but as Pangaea began its main fragmentation around 120 million years ago, many of its fragments (the present Continents) began to drift into much less suitable climatic zones. Clearly the reptile body was moving into a situation where its long-term survival ability was in question. And yet the large reptiles, the dinosaurs, whose bodies were most distinctly vulnerable to climatic change, didn't just gradually begin to die out as the continental masses began to move north or south. They appeared to have died out almost at once.

The answer to this riddle appeared a few years ago, with the discovery of an extremely thin rock layer, which formed around the time of the extinction and which carried large amounts of the element Iridium. Iridium is a relatively rare element on the Earth, and yet here it was found in significant concentrations in what appeared to be a fine ash layer. Although it is relatively rare on the Earth, Iridium is found in significant amounts in meteorites. It appears that the Earth may have been struck by a very large meteorite, or even a small asteroid, throwing an immense amount of dust and debris into the atmosphere. This is not unlike what scientists are forecasting as a 'nuclear winter' in which the smoke and debris from a number of nuclear explosions would throw large amounts of dust into the high atmosphere, reflecting back a significant amount of sunlight into space. This would cause a dramatic temperature drop on the surface of the Earth, which could create winter of several years duration. Even a small asteroid striking the Earth would throw up even more debris than that, and could cause major climatic changes over the entire planet, perhaps lasting for many years.

It would appear that the dinosaurs just died from the cold. With such large bodies, the drop of only a few degrees in body temperature could have been fatal.

A cosmic catastrophe? Or just the Universe's way of creating more durable species?

Extinctions such as this appear at regular intervals, and it is suggested that our Sun may have a companion star in a long orbit around it, that reappears every 26 million years or so, bringing with it a cloud of comets and other debris, some of which collide with the Earth.

Old species die out, and perhaps as a result of seeded life-forms from the debris, new ones may appear. All very speculative at this stage, but a fascinating thought.

At any rate, by the time of the dinosaur extinction, a new evolutionary breakthrough was underway, perhaps once again fuelled by space viruses.

The mammals had arrived.

Because mammals can regulate their own body temperatures, whatever climatic changes took place when the dinosaurs died out were merely an inconvenience to the mammals. And because so many reptilian lines came to an end, there was a great deal less competition for food, so the mammals thrived and developed rapidly. Your most immediate ancestors.

And don't forget, at every stage were the bacteria – modifying, improving, making organic life possible.

We see it everywhere.

The roots of plants, such as peas and beans, would be of no use whatever without masses of rhizobial bacteria incorporating themselves in the root hairs, and providing the chemical reactions necessary to nourish the plant.

Insects have colonies of bacteria living inside them, and functioning as glands; they are absolutely essential to the life of the insect.

The microfloras of animal intestinal tracts (including yours) are a vital part; nutrients could not be released from food without them.

And then there are the mitochondria, the part of the animal cell that is responsible for energy production, and chloroplasts – both individual creatures in their own right, that are present in everything.

A pattern that emerges in biology, is that *the greater the complexity, the greater the vulnerability*. Perhaps when we notice this, the thought will occur to us that as the most complex being, we are also the most at risk. Humankind is the most endangered of all species.

So, who were our most recent ancestors?

The study of the recent biological origins of human beings has been thrown into turmoil lately by the discovery that we are virtually identical genetically to chimpanzees and gorillas.

This discovery by biologists overturns the accepted idea that humankind developed separately from apes in the distant past, more than 20 million years ago, and have thus developed into very different creatures.

A Harvard University anthropologist recently remarked: "We used to think we were the cousins of apes: now it is becoming clear that we are more like brothers and sisters." Paleontologists (scientists who study human fossils) have argued that human ancestory must stretch into the distant past, as human skeletons are very different to ape skeletons. But a recent discovery in China has undermined the paleontologists' case. The evidence comes in the form of the first skull to be found of an early ape-like being called Ramapithecus.

Ramapithecus was thought by paleontologists to have been Man's oldest direct ancestor, dating back at least 15 million years. This was based, however, on the study of relatively few fragments – a few teeth and bones.

But the complete skull has completely overturned that idea, and shows that Ramapithecus was no early human, but was an ancestor of the Orang-utan.

Although there are a great many unanswered questions, the view of the geneticists seems now to be taking precedence over that of the paleontologists.

According to geneticists, humans are genetically closer to chimpanzees, than for example, horses are to donkeys. Such a revolutionary idea is based on experiments carried out by Professor Maurice Goodman. He and other scientists compared proteins and fragments of genes from humans, chimps, gorillas and other apes, and monkeys. In every experiment they got the same result – that chimps, gorillas and humans are virtually identical, genetically and biologically, compared with other apes and monkeys.

This means that humans could only have diverged as a separate species from apes in the very recent past. They base

Fig. 8

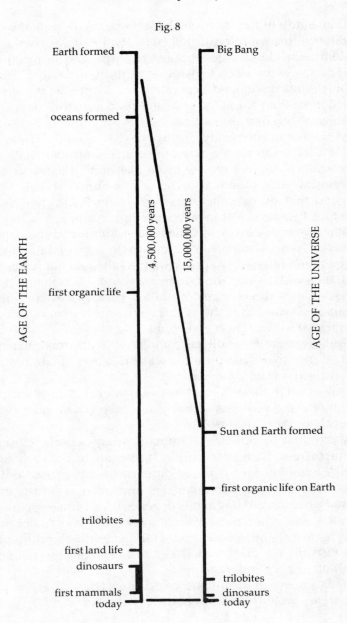

this argument on the assumption that the greater the genetic difference between animals, the further in the past was the date for their divergence from the common ancestor. As a result of their studies, they believe that humanity emerged only about 5 million years ago.

There is only about 1 per cent difference between ourselves and a chimp or a gorilla, and yet that 1 per cent accounts for all of human civilization.

We humans tend to smugly set ourselves apart from the other Kingdoms. And yet you and I are closer to being chimps than chimps are to being monkeys.

Can there be any clearer point to underline our own unity with *all* life on the Earth?

The age relationships of the various stages of development can be shown by two time-lines (see Figure 8). Notice that the age of the human race is too brief to be shown on either line!

The soul evolving through the Kingdoms and the species has many different lessons to learn, all of which add up to the human experience.

In the Mineral Kingdom we learned how to be matter, as opposed to other kinds of energy.

In the Plant Kingdom we began to learn about increasing complexity, and interaction with other species and other Kingdoms.

By the time we have reached the Animal Kingdom, the lessons become much more specific depending on our species capacity. As an example, a soul incarnating as a cat will be learning the lessons of curiosity; and that same soul incarnating as a monkey will be learning about cleverness, and the first glimmerings of self-awareness. And as that same soul moves into human incarnation, the lessons begin to revolve around personality, and indeed, any particular lifetime may see a wide number of lessons and experiences being undertaken.

There are distinct relationships between the various Kingdoms that can clearly be illustrated by a silly example. Silly it may be but I've been using it for years, and I haven't been able to better it.

The first part of the example deals with *free will*. Now, we usually think of free will only in connection with the Kingdom of Man, but as we shall see, it really relates to the number of available choices, which does apply in some degree to the other Kingdoms:

So, the illustration:

M (W)　Kingdom of Man (Woman for you feminists)
A　Animal Kingdom
P　Plant Kingdom
M　Mineral Kingdom

In our illustration, it is a very hot day – too hot. Each Kingdom can experience this to some degree, depending on its capacity for experience. (We might even substitute the word consciousness for 'capacity to experience'.)

And each Kingdom can respond to this situation, relative to its capacity.

In the Kingdom of Man (Woman), we can take off some clothes, sit in the shade, dig a swimming pool, invent the air conditioner, etc., etc., etc. The list is nearly endless. A reflection of capacity/consciousness.

If you are an animal, there are still some choices, but the list isn't so long. You can wallow in the mud, jump in the river, stand in the shade of a tree, or in the shade of a taller animal (this has its own risks). As you can see, it is still a matter of choice, but the list isn't very long.

When we get to the plants, the list is even shorter – roll up your leaves, alter your growth direction, look delicious so a tall animal will stand over you (risky) – still a few choices, but ...

So, we get to the minerals. Choices? None, or maybe one, if it's a *really* hot day. Melt.

This system works okay on the Earth, but what about elsewhere. No plants or animals on the Moon, or Mars (well, maybe a few, but hardly enough to notice). But everywhere we find minerals. For the most part, everywhere *is* minerals.

Minerals – Universal patterns. Patterns that create the Universe.

But no free will. No choice.

And because there is no free will, they are easily influenced by *higher will* acting on them. They can't even say no.

Guess who the higher will is.

Yup.

You and me.

The energies that create the Universe, and they are available to us at our will. Pretty powerful stuff.

Let's look at our silly illustration again and notice a couple more things. Except this time lets look from the bottom up:

(1) The plants use the minerals as a source of raw materials (along with sunlight, another 'inorganic') to create their own bodies.

(2) The animals (I'll let you work out what sort of animal it is) eat the plants, and sometimes other animals who originally ate the plants who originally ate the minerals.

(3) Along comes man(woman) who also eat the plants, and sometimes the animals who ate the plants who ate the minerals.

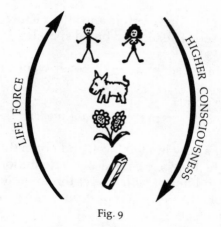

Fig. 9

Getting the idea? It all starts with the *minerals*.

At each stage, the Mineral Kingdom is being incorporated at higher and higher levels of consciousness.

Your own body? Half a bathtub of water (molten ice), and a few cups of powder. Minerals.

You are an evolved mineral.

The biological Kingdoms are just another way of embodying minerals at higher and higher states of consciousness.

If you take a food plant and analyze it chemically, and then go off to your neighbourhood chemical supply store, and mix up the same chemicals, and add in the same amount of water, and then drink it down, how much nutrition is in it?

None.

So if the minerals that make up the plant aren't providing nutrition, what is?

How about Life Force. Or whatever other name you want to call it.

There is a famous experiment with Kirlian photography – take a newly cut leaf, and photograph its 'aura'. Do this every few minutes, and the aura will begin to fade. When it is entirely gone, scientifically analyze the dead leaf alongside a newly cut one. There is no difference – except one has lost its Life Force.

Ever seen any of those before and after pictures of bread that has been blessed. The blessed bread sparkles. Its Life Force is increased.

See a few of these, and you'll never want processed peas again.

What is the point?

That Life Force begins in the Mineral Kingdom.

It is ALIVE.

It is alive at a very limited level, and not in the way we usually define Life. Maybe we need a new definition of Life: *Life is the flow of energy through matter*. Does this exclude the minerals? Definitely not. Run this one past your inner truth detector, and see how it feels.

Remember in Chapter 2 the discussion of Geology, also called How the Earth Lives. Now do you see what that was all about.

And in Chapter 7 there is a discussion about artificial life.

Perhaps you'll find some connections with this section there also.

So then, the Universe is a place that is alive, at many different levels. It has created many minerals in the Mineral Kingdom, and many species in the Plant and Animal Kingdoms. All different ways of experiencing Life.

But until it created You, nothing in the Universe, or at least in our little corner of it, was *self* aware.

4

Union

What exactly *are* we? Thomas says:

"A good case can be made for our non-existence as entities.
We are not made up, as we had always supposed, of succes-
sively enriched packets of our own parts. We are shared,
rented, occupied. At the interior of our cells, driving them,
providing the oxidative energy ... are the mitochondria,
and in a strict sense they are not ours. They turn out to be
separate little creatures ..., probably primitive bacteria that
swam into ancestral ... cells and stayed there. Ever since,
they have maintained themselves and their ways ..., with
their DNA and RNA quite different than ours. Without
them, we would not move a muscle, drum a finger, think a
thought.

Mitochondria are stable and responsible lodgers ... But
what of the other little animals, similarly established in my
cells, sorting and balancing me, clustering me together? My
cells are no longer the pure line entities I was raised with:
they are ecosystems more complex than Jamaica Bay.

I am consoled, somewhat, by the thought that the green
plants are in the same fix. They could not be plants, or
green, without their chloroplasts, which run the photosynthesis enterprise, and generate oxygen from the rest of us.
As it turns out, chloroplasts are also separate creatures ...
speaking their own language."[6]

Well, there it is. We are cities. We are colonies. We are cellular multi-nationals.

Every cell in your body is a separate creature in its own
right. A few million cells that decided to get together and be
you for a while.

How like the Universe we are. If we substitute a few words in the last paragraph, we get something like: a few million stars and planets and organic bits and pieces that decided to get together and be a Universe for a while.

Can you see now how your own body is said to be a microcosm of the Universe?

But with all of this, you are still You, still human.

What then, are the things that make us uniquely human, and how do we experience ourselves and our world as a result?

It is observed that:

"Language is the single human trait that marks us all genetically, setting us apart from all the rest of life. Language is, like nest-building or hive-making, the universal and biologically specific activity of human beings.

We are born knowing how to use language. The capacity to recognize syntax, to organize and deploy words into intelligible sentences, is innate in the human mind. We are programmed to identify patterns and generate grammar. The universal attributes of grammar are genetically set; we do not learn them or make them up as we go along.

If language is at the core of our social existence, holding us together, housing us in meaning, it may be also safe to say that art and music are functions of the same universal, genetically determined mechanism. If we are social creatures because of this, and therefore like ants, I for one ... do not mind."[7]

This means we possess DNA unique to the human – special genetic coding for the *recognition of pattern*. Most, if not all characteristic human behaviour derives from the central mechanism of language, or at least the biological mechanisms that generate language.

This inbuilt ability to recognize pattern is also our strong link to crystals. They are patterns fundamental to the creation of the Universe, and our links with them are therefore a basic part of our own inner, innate nature.

Human behaviour is also linked to pattern. And is a point of connection with the other Kingdoms. But we humans like to think of ourselves as unique individuals, not at all like the grubby animals, and most *certainly* not behaving like horrid insects. Yet, as Thomas observes:

> "Ants are so much like human beings as to be an embarrassment. They farm fungi, raise aphids as livestock, launch armies into wars, use chemical sprays to alarm and confuse enemies, capture slaves. They exchange information ceaselessly. They do everything but watch television.
>
> What makes us most uncomfortable is that they ... seem to live two kinds of lives: they are individuals ..., and they are at the same time component parts, cellular elements; in the huge, writhing, ruminating organism ... of the nest. It is because of this aspect, I think, that we most wish for them to be something foreign. We do not like the notion that there can be collective societies with the capacity to behave like organisms. If such things exist, they can have nothing to do with us."[8]

Yet, like the insects, or even schools of fish, humans do a great deal of collective thinking, although most of it is hardly noticed until you look. In insects and schools of fish, we can see it at work, and we have scientific names for such behaviour. In our own realm, we also have a scientific word for it, although only a few scientists would recognize it.

It is called Fashion.

Its rituals are enacted every spring in places like Paris and London, when the latest articles of collective colouration are displayed. It is enacted in Hollywood in flickering celluloid images, that are one year called Westerns, another year called Sci-Fi, yet another year Musicals.

Other rituals are enacted in obscure locations: in the fifties in Nashville, in the sixties in Liverpool; in the eighties in God God Knows Where.

Other collective rituals are enacted in changing metallic shapes in Detroit, named Ford or Cadillac, or in the re-enactment of other human rituals in the electron tube of the rectangular box deposited in most human nests in the Western world, and increasingly in the Eastern.

Are we so different than the rest of the world we live in after all? The only real difference is that we can *choose*. Choose whether or not to enact any of these rituals, or to change them as we please.

When an insect is doing what his biological nature programmes him to do, such as an ant herding aphids, or a bee making for a flower, it is impossible for that insect to conceive that there might be anything *else*.

But connected in some way with the process of the human mind, is the ability to think about anything *except* what you are doing. And herein lies all of the possibilities of human creativity; for here is the process by which the human mind works out how to do the work at hand even better, or at least differently. We are not 'locked on' to only one way of doing things, and it is here that human progress takes shape. And this is one clue to human societies degenerating – when a society becomes obsessed with preserving the status-quo, it is working against its own best (and biological) interests.

Because we are creatures of more than our own biology, unlike the entire Plant Kingdom, and almost all of the Animal Kingdom, we also have the opportunity to work against our own best interests as a species. You read the newspapers and watch the news on television – do you doubt this for a moment?

It isn't all dark by any means though. As we gain more insight into ourselves, and into the nature of our own being, both personally and as a society, we can start to see the glimmer to new ideas. As we watch the world around us more closely, we see patterns, and more patterns.

One pattern you have possibly experienced might be called 'group energy': the total energy of a group is greater than the sum of its parts.

We even see models for this in nature:

"Termites are extraordinary in the way they seem to accumulate intelligence as they gather together. Two or three termites in a chamber will begin to pick up pellets and move them from place to place, but nothing comes of it; nothing is built. As more join in, they seem to reach a critical mass, a quorum, and the thinking begins. They place pellets atop pellets, then throw up columns and beautiful, curving symmetrical arches, and the ... architecture of vaulted chambers is created."[9]

Humans engage in a similar process of collective thinking. Ziman, in a recent essay in *Nature*, points out:

"The invention of a mechanism for the systematic publication of *fragments* of scientific work may well have been the key event in the history of modern science.

A regular journal carries from one research worker to another the various ... observations which are of common interest .... A typical scientific paper has never pretended to be more than another little piece in a larger jigsaw – not significant in itself but as an element in a grander scheme. This technique ... achieves a corporate, collective power that is far greater than one individual can exert."[10]

If you think about it, this could also describe, in slightly modified terms, the building of a termite nest.

Why should it be a surprise that humans are collective animals? To some degree, every species on the Earth is. And secondly, we are a collective by the very nature of our physical being – a collection of cells.

We know that our mind and our body can be at odds with one another. It is the root of many physical disorders.

Your body has a mind of its own – the collective consciousness of the cells that make it up. When they reach a consensus, it is called intuition. It is the basis of the inner sense of truth, the truth detector I hope all of you still have turned on.

So we get an idea that man is a collective thinker, and

perhaps why it is important. We have even given it a name: Collective Consciousness.

Yet we seem to have a fear of it; a fear of being a cog in a machine, an ant in an anthill.

What are we afraid of? Loss of identity? Loss of self? Or is it a memory? A memory of another collective human society. One that didn't work out too well for many of us.

Atlantis.

There are a lot of memories of Atlantis appearing at the moment. In my courses I have had 100-120 spontaneous recalls of various aspects of Atlantis, but obviously most were oriented toward crystals.

As a scientist I was a bit sceptical at first, even though I had had such memories myself. But a pattern soon began to emerge: four or five major points that appeared in every recall, that were all the same.

What they were is not important for the moment.

What Atlantis was all about *is*.

For many of the advanced souls that began to appear on Earth at the beginning of the Atlantian Period, about 20,000 years ago, it was a first experience of extremely dense matter, which perhaps explains why so many mistakes were made. Remember my own experience of the first contact with the Crystal Deva. The feeling of being crushed by the weight. Others have since had the same experience, and have recalled, as I did, that this is what our first body in Earth incarnation felt like.

Atlantis appears to have been a fairly early experiment in a rather young universe, of beginning to live in and experience relatively high levels of density.

Because crystals are the fundamental building blocks of dense matter, it is natural that a great deal of the experience involving denser levels would directly involve them.

Part of the purpose of Atlantis was to influence the material levels of the Earth Being itself, to infuse denser matter with Higher Consciousness. This was to be accomplished by placing major crystals at certain points of focus of Earth energy.

Because the Earth is in a state of constant change and motion, it is necessary for the essential energies of the Earth to be continually in a state of rebalancing, and the lines of energy flow along which this takes place are often referred to as ley-lines. These are the earth's equivalent of the energy meridians of our own physical bodies, used in acupuncture and acupressure to treat the human body.

In treating the human body by either of these two methods, a critical point on one of the energy meridians is chosen, and either a needle is inserted or finger pressure is used on that point. By a relatively small input of energy at a particularly critical point, results may be produced that affect a great deal of the physical body. A couple of acupuncture needles relative to the mass of the human body is a fairly insignificant amount of matter, and yet placed at a critical point, major effects can be obtained.

Similarly, crystals were placed at certain critical points of earth energy, usually the crossing point of a number of ley-lines, in order to feed higher energies (Higher Consciousness) into the Earth's energy system. And as in acupuncture, a relatively small amount of energy placed in a critical place was able to create effects over a significant portion of the Earth Being. In Figure 10 I have drawn some hypothetical ley-lines on the surface of the earth, and shown how a crystal placed at a critical crossing point could effect a major portion of the surrounding Earth Being. I have drawn the ley-lines as straight lines, although they are not necessarily so. We can observe the tendency of energy to balance itself everyday in our local weather systems. In this instance the flow of energy to create balance is called wind, and it flows from areas of high atmospheric pressures to areas of low atmospheric pressures. Because the movement is quite rapid, combined with the rotation of the earth, it causes rotation of the atmosphere around high and low pressure areas. We would expect a similar effect with ley-line energies, although because the movements take place over a much larger period of time, the tendency to curvature would be very much reduced, but would probably be noticed

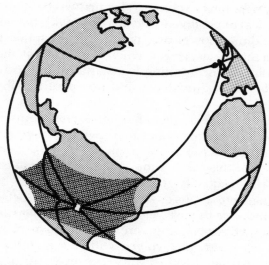

Fig. 10 Hypothetical ley-lines with a crystal in South America. Shaded area is area of crystal energy influence

if we could see a great many miles of the ley-line involved.

One of the major mistakes of the Atlantian Period was in the choice of the crystals themselves, the ones that were used on the major ley-line points. Most memories of this time agree that there were three major crystals, and a number of minor ones that were keyed into those major crystals. But, the major crystals appear to have been brought to the Earth by those who were establishing the Atlantian Civilization, and thus these crystals were not totally attuned to the earth as they were not of the Earth. This lack of complete attunement left some significant gaps in the energy structures that were being linked through them, and as a result of this incomplete attunement, certain manipulations were able to take place of those energies.

This is not to say that the Atlantis experiment was a disaster from the start. Things went well enough for a considerable period (and remember from our early discussion of time, that time itself was a new experience for many Atlantian souls), and a great deal of positive work was done with the Earth.

When the dimension of time is added to the mind, illusion begins to creep in, especially when we focus on the mind rather than intuition. Intuition is instantaneous, and always accurate. No time is involved, and no space for illusion is created.

The thinking mind, on the other hand, is devious and cunning, and will devise strategies to outwit intuition, and even itself, when survival issues are involved.

Because all of this takes 'time', there is plenty of room for illusion – strictly a quality of the conscious mind.

Succeeding generations of Atlantians began to focus on the mind, and distance themselves further and further from their original energetic roots, the core of their own being, and became more and more involved with the material level – often to the virtual exclusion of any other levels. And, because of the illusory nature of much of what occurs on the material level, it was soon enough forgotten by many that there even *were* other levels.

The energetic root of our being is made from three basic parts (perhaps the original concept of trinity?) It forms a triangle, the strongest form in the Universe – as long as all the legs are the same length. If not, it tips over very easily. Just like a personality that has the three parts out of balance. (See Figure 11.)

First, the Power types – you have seen them; you experience

Fig. 11

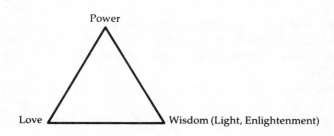

them or read about them every day. People who are full of power, but lack the love to use it properly, or the wisdom to know that by itself power is destruction turned inward. The ruthless businessman, the 'J.R.' type is a classic example of this.

The love-only type is around too. The classic 'hippie' – full of love, but without the wisdom to use his or her power to bring that love into manifestation. They float from place to place with a beautiful smile – 'everything is just wonderful'.

Wisdom by itself? It happens. The Guru on the mountain top is a classic example. Full of knowing, but without the love to bring that knowing down into the market-place.

One of the abilities we have in the dense world is to be *able* to separate these three elements – power, love, and wisdom – into separate components. Perhaps it has been necessary to do so, in order to experience each of them separately at this level; perhaps not. But it happened that way.

The power aspect was what finally got to *us* in Atlantis. Power is often seen as almost a dirty word – but you couldn't walk across the room without the power of your muscles.

It is only when the three elements are not in the right relationship that there is a problem. And so it was with power. Its seductions are well known enough now, when we have had thousands of years to experience it. Imagine what it must have been like then.

Because any society is a composite of all of the individuals in it, the energy fabric of Atlantis began to weaken rapidly, especially with crystals, where so many personal crystals were keyed to the major crystals. Not only were the major crystals themselves not in complete harmony with the Earth, but where individuals were experiencing greater and greater degrees of personal disharmony, there was a great deal of energy feedback through personal crystals to the major crystals, causing even wider gaps of disattunement.

At a certain stage this mounting level of disharmony began feeding back through the devic structure to a great deal of the mineral universe itself, especially to our solar system. And, at the point where it began to upset the delicate balances of the Solar Being, a decision was taken to end the experiment for a while.

At this point, the major crystals were either removed or destroyed, thus much of the energy structure built up over a long period of time was destroyed. This was the direct cause of the Earth changes which brought about the physical destruction of the various land masses that were part of the Atlantian Civilization. (More detail on this period can be found in *Cosmic Crystals*).

This particular period is the root source of much of our personal karma, as a great many advanced souls were on the Earth at the time, but still got caught up in the power aspect. Is it any wonder that there is a hesitation about collective thinking, and collective societies?

Those who carried the pure core of knowledge out of Atlantis became the spiritual roots of many new civilizations throughout the Earth, and many of those civilizations themselves later became involved in the use of crystals. There have been literally hundreds of civilizations that have come and gone in the time since Atlantis, and a very significant proportion of those have been involved with the use of crystals to some degree, either through the use of single crystals or through the use of certain types of rocks which were used for their overall crystalline make-up.

The most significant of these which can still be experienced is the Great Pyramid. The Great Pyramid was intuitively constructed in a crystalline form, with each block of crystalline limestone being oriented as if it were a structural cell in a larger crystal.

We are a collective being, whether we like it or not. Perhaps this is why the Keepers of Wisdom, or the Priesthood, or whatever you want to call them, have for the most part kept themselves isolated from their fellow citizens – to be able to avoid having the pressures of their society placed on them. And to create their own societies (brotherhoods, etc.) that were more in keeping with their inner knowledge.

However it went in Egypt, the capstone was removed, and the pyramid deactivated. We could use another word for this – one we often use with Crystals: de-programmed.

The outer covering and capstone were part of the harmonizing mechanism of the greater whole. It was designed for a specific purpose: it was intended to serve as a doorway into other dimensions; yet the priesthood did not fully understand that the dimensions dwelt within themselves, and the force-field of the Pyramid could only reflect their own inner ability.

Frequently initiation in the Pyramid resulted in the death of the initiate from an inability to survive the self-confrontation that resulted in exploring previously unplumbed depths of the inner being. And, as it was an opening to the inner dimensions of those who survived the experience intact, it served a great purpose for humankind at that time and place.

But, 'instant enlightenment' carries with it its own risks. For if the outer being has not matured sufficiently to handle the discoveries of the inner being, being forced open in this way can lead to serious consequences. In this instance, there was a conscious choice among some of those initiated to use those inner powers and abilities for personal gain, and once again, it began to go wrong.

This is not just a matter of personal maturity either, but cultural maturity as well, for the individual is without a doubt subjected to strong currents from the culture in which he lives.

It was only later on that the ability of the pyramid shape to alter time/space was seen to have a preservative effect on organic materials, that the idea for using pyramids as tombs came into being.

Memories are just re-emerging from many people about how all of this worked, and much of that memory is providing a springboard to a new awakening, and a new and even deeper understanding of it all.

Will it go wrong this time? Only 'time' will tell.

5

Reunion

I am sitting down to write this part of the chapter exactly twenty-four hours after the explosion of the space shuttle Challenger. The crew of Challenger were going about one of the most fundamental of human activities – perhaps as basic to humans as the gathering of pollen to a bee.

The gathering of knowledge and information, and the sharing of that knowledge appears to be an absolutely basic human activity. It is perhaps an extension of language, the one activity that sets us apart from all other species. To be sure, other species pass on learned information – birds have to be taught how to fly, or chimpanzees will teach each other how to use a stick to get at a particularly tasty nest of termites.

And yet no species but the human acquires knowledge simply for its own sake, just for the joy of learning. We know there is a higher purpose behind this, and it is this higher purpose that sets man *uniquely* apart, and is the well-spring of that special joy of new discovery.

Many people returning from near-death experiences report that one of the purposes in 'returning' is to continue to learn and acquire knowledge. To do so often requires risks. But in any lifetime, risks are part of the feeling of 'aliveness', and cultures where risk-taking is frowned upon have a general feel to them of greyness, of lack of 'life'.

This does not imply that we should hurl ourselves in front of buses at every available opportunity, but it clearly says that the more that is risked, the more is gained. This can apply to commerce, to the quest for new knowledge, or especially to the inner quest.

The fears, and therefore the risks, to seeking inner knowledge can be as great as the risks faced by the crew of the Challenger. The body responds in the same way, as if there were a physical danger. The real threat is to old and outmoded ways of thought and belief, which, to the body, can feel as life-threatening as physical danger.

Humans have almost always sought the means to escape or *transcend* the limitations of this physical realm in which they play their part. If as much energy was spent in *transforming* as is spent in attempting to transcend it, we would have long ago made this dimension a holy place. But transcendency is necessary; so we have the paradox of the man who must stand with one foot in dense matter, and one foot in the freedom of his inner infinity. In essence, he must be master of this dimension; but such mastery can only come through the application of the higher love and understanding born in the deepest inner levels of the heart. Discovery of truth does not come about through haphazard events left to chance and whimsy. They are carefully planned, and those who are involved with one another are placed within their life patterns to meet and exchange energy with those who will be most likely to provide the mutual learning experiences. This pre-set pattern often takes the form of training in early childhood, or is associated in early childhood with those people who are most helpful to eventual development and the mission of the soul or souls involved.

In the early days of human history there were many attempts to transcend the limitations of life so that there could be better fulfilment and many different methods evolved; methods of physical, mental and emotional control, training of body energy centres, or training of the mind and intuitive feelings to be sensitized to the presence of the higher truths, often called God.

But, as is often the case, the methods became of greater importance than the goal for which they were evolved, and eventually, the goal itself was forgotten. We are at a time now of the Earth when methodology is falling away, and the inner goals are beginning to emerge once again.

It is the reawakening of the inner self, the higher self, that now begins to respond to the clarion call on a planetary basis.

This thing that we call the New Age, is really nothing more than another turn of the wheel, a re-emergence from the inner darkness, to inner light.

And at the basis of this planetary experience of reawakening are the many courses, methods, and means of personal rediscovery. And all of it oriented toward finding out who we as individuals really are. And all of these methods are oriented toward the shedding away of old patterns, physical, mental and emotional, which distance us from the truth.

And the ultimate goal, of course, is the discovery of the Christ within. Christo Genesis depends on one very important factor; the individual's ability to believe in himself. Without this quality Christ cannot be born. For Christhood is ultimately the pinnacle of self-acceptance, self-trust, and belief and one-ness with the indwelling source. It is within every man upon the Earth.

And as the self awakens other aspects of the surrounding world come into awareness. There is a pattern to this which most human beings seem to be following at the moment; first a higher degree of self awareness – an awareness of one's own thoughts, emotions, and the physical body. Secondly, an awareness of the physical world around us, especially the other Kingdoms of nature – animals, plants, and finally minerals.

Because the Mineral Kingdom exists at the lowest level of consciousness, it is necessary for the re-awakening of the self to have progressed to some extent before the mineral level of energy comes into awareness. A large number of souls on the Earth began again to develop to this stage of awareness around the years 1979-1981, and a second resurgence began to take place in 1984.

Within the courses I was giving at that time, my usual question to each group was "How many of you have just become aware of crystals within the last two years?" In 1980 it was usually two thirds to three quarters of each group had become aware within a two-year period, with the remainder just within the last few months.

That pattern began to change in 1983, with as much as 90 per cent of each group indicating the reawakened interest and awareness only within the last six months. And this accelerating awareness continues to the writing of this book. But why is this reawakening happening, and what ultimately does it mean?

First of all, this reawakening can be seen as a symptom of a large-scale awakening of other levels as well, for as I have said, the awareness of the levels of energy of the Mineral Kingdom only occurs when other levels have already re-awakened. Thus it is a symptom of reawakening at all levels on a global basis. Secondly, with our renewed remembrance and awareness of what went on in Atlantis with crystals, and with some memory, both conscious and unconscious, of the problems, and the potential blessings of them when used as tools of energy, we begin to see that there is a second underlying purpose, which is one of our main reasons for being here: awakening the Earth to higher consciousness.

But the very first stage of this has been to evolve a new view of the world around us; or perhaps to go back to our original view of how the world really is.

We have finally started getting away from the view that the earth is our personal property, to be punched and pummelled and plundered at our own leisure.

I hope you are beginning to see the picture: the Earth is a single, living organism.

It is just like your own body: made up of millions of interacting and mutually dependent components. And most of the components are individuals, even as the cells of your body are individual, but each interacting in a way that provides the greatest opportunity for mutual survival.

You are part of the cellular structure of the Earth Being. Human beings might even be the brains of the earth, although we could find reasonable cause to doubt it.

When a cell of your own body begins to be self-centered, taking only in regard to its own needs, and ignoring those of its neighbour, we call it *cancer*.

Does this description match any people you know?

This doesn't mean that one's needs should not be fulfilled, or that the other Kingdoms of the Earth should not provide for those needs. You *are* those Kingdoms – the Mineral Kingdom provides the chemical building blocks; the Plant Kingdom provides the oxygen to energize those building blocks, as well as the stored energy of sunlight as fuel for the oxygen; and the Animal Kingdom, especially at the microscopic level, provides the building blocks that create your own body and its systems: those few million cells that decided to be *you* for a while.

When you take from the environment you are only taking from yourself – and that is not a bad thing, as long as you do so in harmony with that environment. The mineral-biological world we live in is a system of energy exchange and movement – and energy moving throughout structure is called LIFE.

As reflected on earlier, we are beginning to reawaken our social nature. Not in the sense of 'socialize', but in the sense of our deep interconnection with other humans, and with all life.

We have common ancestors, common patterns, common purpose. This doesn't mean that we have to give up being individuals. The fact that we exist as individuals says that this is how things should be. If we were not meant to be – it would have been created so. And in the next chapter, we discover why we *must* be individuals.

But this doesn't mean that this is *all* we must be. A man once said "Render unto Caesar ...", and so it is with you and me. We share that which is shared, and keep to ourselves that which is uniquely ours.

As we reawaken to the true nature and purpose of humanity in ourselves, we can take assurance from the fact that this is happening in many others as well, all over the Planet, and even more, *exactly the same thing is happening for every one.*

The pattern is the same: first of a sense of "is this all there is?"; then a growing awareness that there *is* more – a 'chance' discovery of a book, an overheard conversation, a friend suddenly surprising you by being 'into' the Spiritual. Then a

growing inner awareness, reflected in a growing outer awareness. New friends are attracted, those who are 'into' the same
sort of ideas that are dawning in you. And old friends left
behind, and dropping away. Then a point where you question
your own sanity – is any of this real?

Then the breakthrough into the psychic level, which we
mistake at first for spirituality. In this level we usually create
some powerful illusions for ourselves, being no longer bound
at this level by the limitations of time: everything is urgent,
everything has to be done *now*. We find the stirrings of past-
life memories, many of us become 'channels' for discarnate
entities. And especially, memories of Atlantis begin to reap-
pear. Of crystals, and power, and of ultimate destruction. The
soul doomed to wander the Earth through many incarnations,
to repair the damage: the roots of our karma.

But sooner or later we begin to break free of the limitations
of the psychic, seeing that it is only another way to feed the
mind. We move into a state of intuition, another name for
inner connection. We learn to trust the feedback our body
gives us, to trust our *feelings*. And soon enough we release the
need for explanation that characterizes the psychic level; the
need to have everything in words. No more trips to the 'Spirit
Guides' at every crisis; we learn to look inside ourselves and
see how it *feels*.

Before long we realize that there is always just enough time
– that the need to rush no longer exists. The inner sense will
say very clearly what needs to be done, and when. Then the
mind becomes our tool, rather than our master. We feed the
mind – but it is insatiable. It is the nature of the human mind
to gather information; in this quest it is mindless. But information can quickly obscure knowledge.

Einstein once said that knowledge is what you have left over
when you have forgotten everything you have learned in
school.

Knowledge is an essence. And the rational side of the brain is
not equipped to deal with essence – only information. To be
sure, one side of the brain feeds the other. But it is the balance

between the two, their right relationship that we seek.

Much of what we are remembering and being told about crystals falls into the category of information. What we really seek is knowledge. To a Western mind, the distinction between the two can be difficult.

If there is one thing I fervently wish to teach you about crystals, it's this: *don't* THINK *about crystals,* FEEL *about them.* Just like everything else you encounter in your life.

This was where the breakdown occurred in Atlantis. We discovered our thinking minds – available to us in this newly created primate body in a way not experienced before. And we stopped feeling about our crystals and our work with the Earth, and started just thinking. We began to serve ourselves to the exclusion of others; if you've forgotten, this is the biological definition of cancer.

I said a few paragraphs ago that Atlantis was the root of much of our personal *karma*. What is karma, exactly?

It is often described as cause and effect. If I do a certain thing, it will have a certain result. The ancients interpreted this as "an eye for an eye".

Looking at it another way, karma is simply a restatement of the basic law of energy: it always has to balance.

Put even simpler: "You gotta clean up your own mess." or even better: "You have to finish your experiences." You'll see how this works out in the next chapter, in the part on soul patterns.

So, a large part of what we are remembering about our own relationships to other Kingdoms, and the crystals of the Mineral Kingdom in particular, is of a time, and of methods of working with crystals, that were absolutely against our own best interests, both as biological organisms, and as receptacles of higher consciousness.

At the moment, many are switching back into those old patterns as the memories reemerge. Few recognize what is happening, because they haven't reached beyond those patterns. We are actively recreating Atlantis.

We cannot, for the moment, do anything *else*. Until our

learning and experience progress beyond the point where we left off, we *must* pick up at the same place.

That we shall do so is not a vain hope, however, for we have not stood still since Atlantis. We have accumulated bits and pieces both as individuals, and collectively, so the journey back to, and the move through the old patterns can be a rapid one.

There are volumes of 'channelled' information available at the moment that might be collectively entitled: "how we did it with crystals in Atlantis."

We did.

But *should* we have?

That is the question that only our continuing experiences of crystals will tell us. We can be absolutely sure of one thing: because Atlantis was a civilization energetically built around crystals, and that civilization not only failed to survive, but was destroyed, in many cases the answer to "Should we have?" is *NO*.

What is it about crystals then? Why do they work, and what do they do?

By themselves, *nothing*.

A crystal is a tool, like a hammer. But a tool for energy. Left alone, the hammer drives no nails; left alone, the crystal does the same – nothing. Tools only 'do' something when there is an input of human energy – with a hammer, muscle power; with a crystal, the power of human consciousness.

And what a power, the human mind. We tend to not notice it, because it is so commonplace. But the next time you are in the middle of a city, or somewhere that is filled with the products of human endeavour, just look around and really *see*: every single man-made thing around you began as an idea, a thought.

You, as a human being, have, through your body with its ability for mobility (legs) and manipulation (hands) a complete 'creation system'. An ability to formulate an idea, and translate that idea into form. Only one other being in the Universe can do that.

God.

If your mind is linked to the Universal mind, whatever you create while linked to that mind is a direct outworking of that mind. Maybe that is why teachers have always said that we should always do everything we do in the world in our own highest state of consciousness. It doesn't matter whether we are stamping out hubcaps on an assembly line, or working with crystals. It is *all* an act of the Spirit.

What about crystals? We have established that they are tools of energy, and that they need human input to function.

Remember in an earlier chapter we talked about our very human ability to recognize patterns. It is this ability that is our link to crystals, which in themselves are atomic patterns (fourteen of them, remember).

You have your own pattern of course, – your soul pattern. And this is what makes you unique. We'll look at some patterns specifically in the next chapter, but for now let's just remember another Cosmic law: *like attracts like.*

Ever wonder why you are attracted to one crystal among hundreds of seemingly identical ones? Like attracts like. Your soul pattern recognizes a like pattern in a particular crystal.

But there are only fourteen aren't there?

True. But the inner pattern is not quite all there is to the make-up of an individual crystal. The outer pattern of faces is generated by the inner atomic pattern, but the final outer dimensions of the crystals are strictly a product of the growth environment. A crystal an inch long, although having an identical inner and outer pattern, will have a *total* energy make-up different from a crystal two inches long.

What makes the difference?

Resonance.

The way energy 'bounces around' inside a crystal.

Resonance is fundamentally governed by the atomic structure, giving a somewhat similar pattern for each crystal. But the overall physical dimensions, including the development of various faces on the crystal, will change the overall 'character' of the crystal. Making it an individual.

It's not unlike you. You and I are alike in most ways physically. One of those, two of these, one of that. And so on. Our cells are alike, our skeletal structure has the same number of bones in the same position, and so on. So what makes us different? Our total energy make-up. Just like crystals.

Ever wonder why when you pick up a crystal 'cookbook' and it says do this thing with that particular type of crystal, it often doesn't work? It worked for the person who gave you the recipe, so why doesn't it work for you?

You aren't that person, and you aren't using their crystals.

Even if you did use their crystals, the very crystals they were writing about, probably nothing would happen for you. Their crystals would most likely not be attuned to your energy, so nothing happens.

How do you know which crystals are yours?

Feel them.

If you get a 'feels right' feeling, you're there.

The technologists among you may want to choose your crystals by doing mathematical computations of the various parameters of the crystals you are drawn to ,to see if there is a common denominator. Why not. I'd be interested to know myself, but I'm too lazy to work it out myself.

Resonance, by the way, is what makes pyramids do what they do. The angles of the faces tend to focus energy at a certain point inside the pyramid. Certain angles, such as the Great Pyramid angle, focus the energies in such a way that they cancel to a degree, creating a space inside where the rules of time/space are altered. This is why they were created in the first place.

So, in the preceding chapters we have looked at the human organism – mind, body and spirit. We begin to see that the individual human being is part of a larger organism – humankind. That humankind is a part of an even larger organism – the Earth. One of four Kingdoms that collectively make up the Earth Being.

And that humankind, through a unique set of abilities, is part of the conscious connection of the Earth to its Universe;

we are an integral part of its capability as a Being for Self-awareness.

Let's remember the beginning of all things, and remind ourselves of the bottom line: it's all energy. Energy just arranged in different patterns.

Your own life is about energy patterns too. In the next chapter, we'll look at those patterns, and see how those patterns relate to crystals – those fundamental patterns of all creation.

6

Circles

The human body is an energy system, containing in itself all of the characteristics of the Universe. There is embodied in it a hierarchy of energies, one grading into the other, with certain points of focus at the major levels.

These points of focus are called *chakras* (Figure 12), and are the energetic framework upon which the physical body is hung. Each of these points has an energy correspondence in the other Earth Kingdoms, except for the seventh, your connection with the Cosmos.

Fig. 12 General location of the seven chakras

The lowest two are connected with (and are part of) the Mineral Kingdom, the dense material aspect of your body; the next two to the Plant Kingdom, to the external awareness aspect; and the last two to the Animal Kingdom, to the part of yourself where inner awareness begins to take form, and merge with outer awareness. And the last, to connect you at a conscious and choice level to the universal mind (or God, the IS, the Universal Mind, Brahma, the Tao, or whatever). In a sense, this is the energy centre that is the most *Yours*. The other centres come automatically with a physical body, and more or less run themselves.

Think not?

How would you like the job of running your own pancreas?

Do you know what it does? Even if you do, do you know how to make what it makes, and know when to send it off to wherever it goes? Best to just get out of the way, and leave the pancreas to get on with it. The micro-organisms that designed your body and then took over its running have had a lot of practice – about 3 thousand million years.

The biggest problem is in staying out of their way, and letting them get on with it.

Unlike most other creatures, we have the ability to go against our own nature, and our own best interests, and we frequently choose to do so. We have talked about this earlier in relation to the outer environment. It is also true of the inner environment, that complex series of beings that is you.

The seventh chakra is plugged into the Universal you, but you can choose to pull the plug any time you wish (I've often described free will as nothing more than the ability to say *no* to your own divinity): it is easy to break the circle. Remember, energy always balances, and it always travels in circles. It looks like this:

Fig. 13

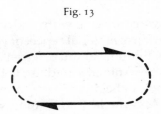

For every action there is an equal and opposite reaction: energy always moves in a circle.

Any time the circle is broken, a blockage appears. The flow of energy in the human would look something like this:

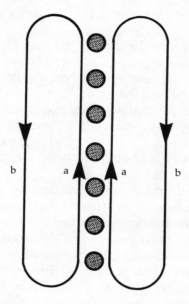

Fig. 14 Energy through the chakras

On the 'a' side, Earth energy is being elevated through the chakras to the seventh, the Divine. On the 'b' side, Divine (the other word I like is Universal) energy is being passed into the earth by moving down the chakras. At each energy level, each chakra there is feedback into the corresponding Kingdom.

This does not imply that each Kingdom has the same experience as the Human – only that they experience that level of energy according to their own capacity.

As I have been saying through the book, choice goes with complexity. In the Mineral Kingdom, although there is great order, there is little complexity. In the Plant Kingdom, complexity increases, and so does choice.

With the Animal Kingdom, complexity increases considerably, especially as the brain gets more complex; likewise the choices get greater. Remember the 'hot day' example in Chapter Three.

In studies of animal behaviour, we begin to notice that the animals with brain capacity nearest to ours begin to develop some very human characteristics. Not so much in the way they behave, but in the way they *react*.

Have you ever noticed how pets, generally animals of relatively higher capacity, behave in certain households. In fact, aren't they more or less a mirror of what goes on?

Neurotic household, neurotic pets; well-adjusted household, happy pets.

Mistreat a pet and it may well develop almost identical behaviour to a human mistreated in the same way. True, many of the human defences will be verbal, but take this away and watch the body language – it is the same.

Even plants reflect our own personalities. Most of you are probably familiar to some degree with research into plants, and their ability to sense and respond to human thought. Especially striking is their response to aggressive or hostile human behaviour – an electrochemical scream.

Is any of this a surprise though? Most of us know how life works: the world around us reflects ourselves back to ourselves all the time. Like attracts like. Like *recognizes* like. It's all pattern recognition, the basic human characteristic.

But what patterns are we recognizing?

Ours.

Our own deepest inner patterns. Call it the soul if you like – the soul pattern.

In immensely deep meditation in the heart centre, a pattern begins to emerge: many I have talked to have had exactly the same experience. I have had it myself.

The inner core of the being (the soul) is a pattern of light. It looks something like this:

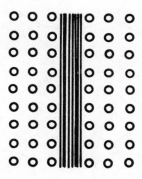

Fig. 15 Soul pattern

It is always described as being made of bluish light, and is a series of dots forming a regular pattern around a central core (the deepest core of the being?).

Each dot is an experience. To complete the soul pattern, each dot must be complete.

To graduate from the Earth, fill in the dots. Simple as that.

In a sense this inner pattern is like a crystal – a regular pattern of energy. And, your pattern is part of a larger pattern – the Group Soul. The Group Soul is in turn part of an even larger pattern, often referred to as a Spiritual brotherhood – and so on until the largest pattern: the Universe. At each stage, energy is stepped down, until we reach the material plane.

This is the basis for your mission on the Earth. Your mission is *self-completion*. As you can see, the connection is not complete, the overall pattern is not complete, until *you* are. Until you complete yourself (fill in the dots), the *Universe* is not complete.

Fig. 16

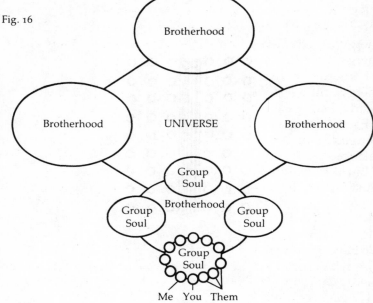

It has been said that the best gift you can give the world is a whole you. Now do you see why?

And now do you see why you are unable to change the world without first changing yourself? *You* are what is getting in the way.

So what is getting in *your* way?

Fear. Always. More on that later.

There are a lot of excellent personal development courses around at the moment, and it is not the purpose of this book to try and be one. But rather to give a perspective on how your own inner development is a vital part of the process of the Universe itself.

So how do you start? First, it helps to understand a bit more about what you are.

It all ties into patterns (surprise, surprise!)

Your own inner pattern, the pattern of experiences, is, as I have said, an energy pattern. Why an energy pattern though?

Because everything in the Universe is energy. Not just energy as matter, but energy as thought, energy as emotion, energy as experience. An experience *must* be some type of energy, because *everything* is.

I know I'm hammering this point of everything being energy, but when we really understand, it helps to see things clearly, because it is all so simple.

Each dot is an experience – each experience is energy; therefore each experience must obey the laws of energy. Circles and balance.

But this also implies an exchange of energy, since energy must flow both ways. We could draw this as a circle:

 As you experience a thing
so a thing experiences you

We have another name for exchange of energy: *relationship*.

A relationship could be thought of as the *quality* of the energy exchange. If energy is exchanged with one quality to it, it is called an atom.

If energy at a different level, a different quality, is exchanged, it is called a marriage. Energetically, there is no difference between an atom and a marriage; only the qualities of the exchange are different.

Energy is also exchanged between different levels. In fact, energy is in constant motion, in a series of constantly changing relationships. What was your relationship to this book on page 1? On page 50? Now?

The Universe is a place made of energy relationships, not of things.

Your own inner pattern, then, is made of relationships, more specifically, how you relate to the events which take place in your life. Events are created in your life by you in order to establish what, for you, is your right relationship to those events. When you establish your right relationship (according to your own inner pattern), you are said to have 'learned the lesson'.

You are not alone in this quest. You have with you at all times, your inner connection to your own Group Soul.

One of the functions of the Group Soul is to aid all of its members, and there may be hundreds or even thousands, to completion. Obviously; because completion at the Group level is the mission of the Group Soul, and this cannot happen without the completion of all of its members.

If your immediate need is to see things in terms of separation, you will see members of your Group Soul as separate beings from you. You will often experience them as 'Spirit Guides', or 'Guardian Angels'. They are really part of you. A medium's 'source' will also be part of the Group Soul. The medium is really just 'channelling' himself, at a different level. But because it is filtered through the personality, channelling *always* has inbuilt flaws.

Right. So that's what's going on energetically.

So how does it work in practice?

You have heard of 'karmic relationships'. Most of you are in them now. Others of you are looking for your soul mate, or your twin soul.

Your soul mate is anyone who can help you work through the lessons you have chosen for this lifetime.

The energy circle looks like this:

⟨   As you experience your partner
    your partner experiences you   ⟩

No doubt many of you will draw to yourselves the persons you have worked with before. Look at it this way:

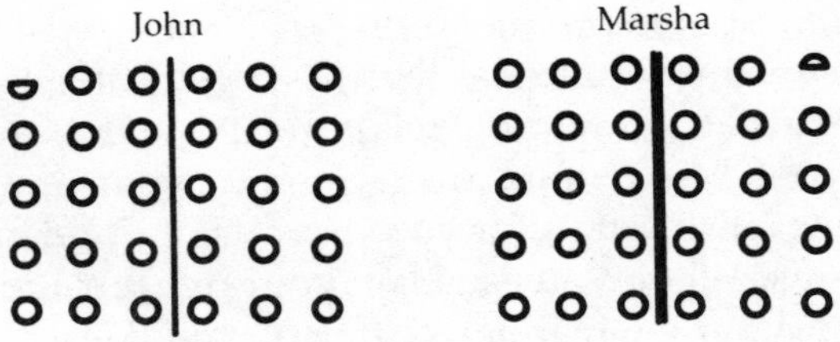

Fig. 17 John & Marsha

The soul pattern of John has an incomplete experience in row 1, position 6. Marsha has not completed the other half of the same experience, but in position 1 of row 1. The experiences interlock. The energy flow is complete, and moving in a circle. The laws of energy are satisfied. John and Marsha, for this experience at least, are 'soul mates'.

Those who study the dynamics of relationships on a psychological level call this an 'interlocking relationship'. All do to some degree. The strength of attraction we feel for our opposite is an indication of how much mutual incompleteness there is; of how much is to be learned from the relationship.

If this attraction is between a man and a woman, it is conventionally called 'love', or 'romantic love'. If it is between members of the same sex, it is conventionally called 'friendship'. This is a convention that is clearly breaking down at the moment. Who cares, as long as the lessons are learned.

When the energetic attraction for completion is strong enough, a formal commitment is often made between the two people involved to stay together until the lessons are learned. This commitment is called 'marriage'.

But if John completes 90 per cent of his lessons, and Marsha only finishes 20 per cent and refuses to learn more the energetic bond is often broken, so each partner can find someone else who is learning at the same rate. John will match someone new who is working on the same lesson at a complementary energy level, and so will Marsha. They have each found a new 'soul mate'. Breaking, or really acknowledging that the old bond no longer exists is called 'divorce'.

It is all governed by the laws of energy, and all oriented toward completing the soul pattern.

Incidentally, it is not necessary for John and Marsha to come from the same Group Soul. But as the Group Soul is working on an overall lesson that is part of John and Marsha's lessons, it is frequently so. It is particularly true in intense relationships, where there are a lot of lessons going on at once. When there is also a recognition that the other person is part of your own Group Soul, it is often called 'love at first sight'.

Now if John and Marsha were working on a series of lessons in another lifetime, and the relationship was interrupted by the death of one partner (some people will get out of finishing lessons at all costs), if neither of them has progressed beyond the point where they left off, then it is natural that they would be attracted in a later lifetime. They have both left their maturative lessons at the same point, and there is a perfect energy match.

What is it exactly that causes unfinished lessons?

It is always fear. And it always causes a blockage in the body's energy systems. *An energy block is just an unfinished lesson.*

Remember the definition of fear: the body's way of protecting itself from a perceived danger. It is a *body* reaction, not a mental one. It is the collective decision of all those parts that make up you, that its survival is at stake. The chemical secretions that we interpret as fear is the body preparing to defend itself. The secretions come first, and then our thinking minds take note of them. Somewhere a few neurons in the brain flash on.

"Neuron 231207 to neuron 16276: I sense adrenalin."

"Neuron 16276 to neuron 37154: adrenalin means fear."

"Neuron 37154 to cerebral cortex: fear present; there must be a danger."

What has triggered the production of adrenalin in the first place? A pattern has been recognized:

At age 3:   Mother (woman) raises voice = loss of life support system = threat to survival = body prepares to meet threat = adrenalin (fear).

At age 33:   Wife (woman) raises voice = withdrawal of support = loss of life support = threat to survival = body prepares to meet threat = adrenalin (fear).

The body, or really the *body's mind*, the subconscious, has recognized a pattern, and triggered what it believes to be an appropriate response to that pattern. There may have been a genuine threat at the time the pattern was established – withdrawal of support from a three-year-old *is* life threatening. But as an adult, the same body responses are *not* appropriate. The right relationship to events has been lost. The lesson? Re-establish the right relationship.

These patterns that are established in childhood are always a result of the soul pattern, and are the lessons we have chosen for this lifetime.

Why childhood?

Because this is the time when we set up for ourselves, along with our chosen set of parents, the events that establish the lessons. They are already there, in the energy state of the soul pattern, when the soul attaches to the forming embryo. Because we have chosen to learn on the material level (our incarnation on the Earth is evidence of that), we must recreate our patterns on the physical level.

The patterns are quickly established in our body energy centres – the chakras – as energy blocks. These blocks are established in the physical body as early as possible, either in the womb or through traumatic childhood events. We almost always take on only what we can handle at any stage. If we take on more than we can handle, we just leave the body and don't come back. We die, and come back to try it again: with a little less trauma next time.

Someone once said that all parents are meant to fail. If they didn't, there would be no lessons for you to learn. Moreover, the depth of their failure is a measure of how much you have chosen to learn this time around.

There is another early type of pattern that is very much an energy pattern: a habit pattern. Most of our ways of thinking and acting are habitual.

Do you ever wonder why it seems to take such a long time to break a habit?

Look at it energetically: suppose you develop a habit when you are 10 years old. Each year of your life you put one unit of energy into your habit pattern. When you are 20 years old, you decide to break the pattern. At that point your habit has accumulated ten energy units. So, to balance the energy, you must also put out ten units to break it. But if you try to break it in a year, it is taking *ten times* as much energy to break it as it did to form it (at the rate of one unit per year).

Sometimes it seems to take forever to create change in your life – now you see why. Now you also know the meaning of the old saying: "Old habits die hard."

Of course, this is the reason why many personal development courses are designed the way they are: to shatter old patterns quickly by producing a great deal of energy all at one time, usually emotional, and providing the means to safely release it. The process is called catharsis.

Throughout, you are being constantly reminded of your own patterns by what the world around you reflects back to you. The world is designed to give you constant feedback about who you are, and what you are at any particular moment.

There is another circle related to this that I have found helpful to me:

ARE

YOU   (YOU)   NOT

OHM

Let me put it in words: very often you find out who you are, by being who you are not.

How many things have you tried in your life, only to one day realize "This isn't me". And if anyone had asked you in that moment "So who are you then?", could you have given them an answer? It's as if we go through life trying this and trying that, only to discover that they are not quite 'it'. What is left over in the middle is *me*. And that doesn't require a definition. *I* am not a this, or a that or the other. *I* am a state of *being*. And that doesn't require defining. I may *do* this or that or the other, but what I *do* is not what I *am*.

True, it is a reflection of what I am, but a reflection is not the thing itself.

Now, if I feel the further need to re-define my own experience of myself (make the circle smaller), I usually step out of my state of *being* back into a state of *doing*. I step back into who I am not – which gives me a more focussed sense of who I am. It's just that as the circle gets smaller, I don't have so far to step. (And what a relief *that* is.)

Remember how the dinosaurs died out suddenly? I sometimes wonder if the Universe, in its quest for self-discovery, didn't look at the dinosaurs one day, and say: "*that's* not me."

What has any of this got to do with crystals? Remember that we are dealing with *patterns* of soul growth, and the human mind is biologically created to recognize patterns; secondly that the world around us is created to reflect ourselves back to ourselves. Because crystals are always perfect patterns (and if they weren't, they wouldn't be crystals), they also give perfect reflections. Perfect reflections back to you of your own perfect patterns – and by contrast your imperfect ones.

Almost the first word that comes to mind when crystals are mentioned is *healing*. Healing is probably the most over-used word in the whole 'alternative' movement. Most of what we call healing, isn't. To a large extent, 'healers' have done very little that is different from orthodox medicine: the relief of symptoms.

Remember what disease often is in a biological sense: your body's reaction to viruses and bacteria that are trying to alter your genetic pattern. It's your body's way of saying "no, thanks".

Thomas remarks:

"The great secret, known to internists and learned early in marriage by internists' wives, but still hidden from the general public, is that most things get better by themselves. Most things, in fact, are better by morning."[11]

He continues:

"Our arsenals for fighting off bacteria are so powerful, and involve so many different defense mechanisms, that we are in more danger from them than from the invaders .... We are minefields."[12]

"We are paying too little attention, and respect, to the built-in durability and sheer power of the human organism. It is a distortion ... to picture the human being as a teetering, fallible contraption, always needing watching and patching, always on the verge of flopping to pieces ... We ought to be ... developing ... better education ... about human health, ... and even some celebration of the absolute marvel of good health that is the real lot of most of us, most of the time."[13]

"The man who catches a meningococcus is in considerably less danger for his life ... than a meningococci with the bad luck to catch a man.

Meningococci are not at all uncommon – during epidemics most of the population will have them. It is only in the tiny minority of cases that the immune systems of a few people will react to them – and these people are said to be ill."[14]

Staphylococci live everywhere on our skins – and yet few of us have any sort of reaction whatever to them. A few people do develop boils – but these are mostly a result of 'overkill' on the part of their own immune system.

What does all of this show us? For one, it says that because we are 'ill' it doesn't necessarily mean there is anything *wrong* with us.

Your immune system is specifically designed to reject any genetic changes that are not part of your pattern. That sort of 'illness' is perfectly normal. But if your immune system is weakened by stress (and it is usually one of the first things affected), then your body has to put a lot more of its energy into rejecting foreign bacteria or viruses.

You become 'ill' more easily.

How do we deal with that? We can pump ourselves full of drugs – or we can go to a 'healer' to get our body energies pumped up again for a while. But have we been *healed*? Of course not. We haven't dealt with the source of our 'illness' – the patterns which generate stress. Our 'illness' is a *symptom*. A reflection of inner patterns out of kilter. Most of us need our 'illnesses' – they are good reflections of our inner processes.

So, to stop feeling 'ill', fix the inner, not the outer.

How?

Crystals are not the answer. They may be *part* of it, but they are not the most important factor.

You are in this world to *relate*. To the world around you, but especially to other people. Almost all of our 'filling in the dots' toward soul completion is about human relationships. And anything inside you that is a barrier to this is a barrier to your own completion – and a source of 'illness'.

Nothing will change until you take action to change yourself.

Often what happens, though, is when we decide to make some real changes in ourselves, we get on to a 'spiritual' path – we think we are making progress. And fear comes up. So at first, we mostly give ourselves even better excuses to stay as we are: "spiritual people don't get angry" – so you never have to deal with your anger. "Spiritual people are always positive" – so you never have to deal with your own doubts. And so on. We often mistake piety for spirituality.

As we move into the psychic levels of awareness it's like being born again. A new world opens, and we forget how confusing the *old* one was at the start.

Because the psychic level is relatively timeless, everything is *now*. We forget that the processes of the Earth are slow and steady. You don't plant a crop on Wednesday and harvest on Thursday.

We get into Service – and forget that the best way to avoid having to deal with your own mess is to deal with everyone else's.

Then we discover crystals: we see them as the Cosmic Cavalry coming to save the Earth – a great blowing of horns, as if the True Messiah had suddenly appeared. The Great Cosmic Father, here to relieve us of our responsibility for our own lives, and the mess we have made from our own irresponsibility.

But somewhere while on this sort of high, a light flickers on:

You can't change the world around you until you change yourself. That's the only way it works.

Such is the *real* power of human creativity: the power to change yourself.

The Master is only master of himself.

I might just make a note here on 'negativity' or 'the forces of darkness' or 'evil'. I tend to think of these as just 'in harmony' or 'not in harmony'. If you are struggling in yourself, you may well externalize this as a battle between the forces of light and dark, good and evil. For you, it is. We all have the capacity for both. We embody both. To the extent you fail to embody 'light', dark appears. But it is not a *presence*, it is an *absence*. That is why it has no power of its own, and must always resort to external devices.

So, using crystals to clean up 'dark ley-lines' or 'do battle for the forces of light', is mostly a waste of time. If you experience these things, then ask yourself what is incomplete in you, that which you project as 'darkness'.

There is another circle connected with crystals:

      As you experience a crystal
         the crystal experiences you

Precisely what is it in a crystal that 'experiences'. At the material level, I am certain that we are influencing the sub-atomic structure. It may be a slight shift in the angle that a photon is bound to an electron; it may be that a quark rolls slightly to the left – but something happens.

If you ever have the chance to hold a synthetic crystal, see how it feels. Or even better, hold it in one hand and a natural one in the other. In courses, over 90 per cent will say that the natural one feels 'alive'. I use two quartz crystals – not that quartz is any different from any other mineral; I just happen to have a synthetic quart' crystal. To most, the synthetic feels life-less, clinical, rather like the laboratory in which it was grown. This is a dramatic demonstration that we *can* change the con-sciousness of matter by its contact with us. Both crystals are quartz – absolutely identical mineralogically to one another.

Yet the synthetic feels like a lump of glass. In the case, consciousness is changed by the laboratory environment to feel like a laboratory. Sterile.

This is why I said earlier, it doesn't matter whether it's hubcaps or crystals you are working with – give it your best shot.

Another energy circle is a direct extension of the last one:

As you experience the Earth's crystals
So the Earth experiences you

Once I finally 'got' that the crystal was experiencing *me*, I soon realized that all the other like crystals in the Earth were connected to mine through the Devic force. The linking was through the crystal's energy pattern.

Because the Earth is mostly crystalline (99.99 per cent), its self-awareness must, to a large degree, centre on crystals.

My next realization was even more powerful.

Whatever we did with crystals, we were teaching the earth through them. And to a large degree, as long as we were working from our own inner sense of appropriateness, it didn't matter *what* we did.

Those who were using them for meditation were teaching the earth about higher consciousness. Those who were healing were teaching the Earth about compassion. Those who just loved them for their beauty were teaching the Earth about just that: love and beauty. And I also realized that when I took a crystal from the Earth, I was sharing the whole world outside of the Mineral Kingdom with it.

I had one of my most moving moments a while back in regard to that. I was digging out a vein of quartz crystals – not shiny and sparkly like you see them, but covered with sticky red mud that had filled in the vein at a later time.

As I wiped the mud away, the sun shone through the crystal.

And it hit me: this was the first sunlight this crystal had experienced since it was created 45 million years ago. After 45 million years, *I* had shown it the Sun.

I have come to realize that this is one of my own personal

connections to the learning processes of the Earth – to bring crystals new-born into the world from the womb of the Earth.

I'm often asked if it is all right to remove crystals from the Earth; is it harmful to the Earth?

The Deva:

"A gift from a lover always has a very special meaning, even if it is only an insignificant thing. As long as you take my gifts and accept them from me in the same state of mind as you accept a gift from a lover, then I am well and truly pleased in the giving of my gift."

7

Spirals

A spiral is a circle to which the dimension of time has been added. As we have discovered, time is a property of matter, and is the element of relationship that creates experience. Let me say it another way: energy exchange (relationship) over a period of time creates experience.

The element of time in our reawakening awareness of ourselves and the Universe around us, creates a spiral path. Because experience (time) has passed, we return to the same events and patterns, but further along the spiral.

There is a major circle operating through the Kingdoms that we have, as human beings, the creative capability to turn into a spiral. It is one of the things we are here on the earth to do. You have seen it before.

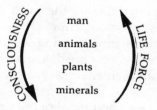

Life Force (energy flow) begins in the Mineral Kingdom. Minerals provide the building blocks of the plants (water, mostly), and the gaseous phase of minerals (the Sun) provides the photons to be converted by the chloroplasts.

We have already looked at how we can influence the Earth's minerals – through crystals. If we elevate the consciousness of the Mineral Kingdom through its contact with us, then all Kingdoms which embody it – and that is all of them, including us, are elevated in consciousness through their mineral nature.

We have created a spiral.

To be sure, the embodiment of the Mineral Kingdom as part of your own body will have some effect by its experience of being you anyway. We process a very tiny amount of the minerals this way, however.

Do you have any idea how much mineral matter the human race embodies? If we take an average human body as fitting into a box 1 foot deep, 1.5 feet wide, and 6 feet high, how much volume do you suppose the entire human race fills?

A cube about half a mile on a side.

And over 90 per cent of that is water. About enough to keep London or New York in water for a couple of weeks or so in a hot summer.

Yet look at the changes wrought on the face of the earth by that lake of water and mound of chemicals embodied in the human race. Can you doubt the *power* of just being human?

This also gives us an idea of how a relatively small portion of the human race can positively affect the world around us. As we develop our own inner clarity, and work with the earth from clarity, we get powerful results. Clear intentions get clear results – if you have no real intentions, you get no real results. Those who attempt to influence the Earth in a positive way do so mostly through conscious effort. Those who are less than helpful to the Earth are mostly doing so through ignorance or short-sighted stupidity. Few are deliberately trying to damage the Earth; as a result their energies are random and much less focussed.

Humankind is the embodiment of the Creative Force on the Earth. I hope you have seen that now.

Emphasis thus far has been largely on *being*. Creativity depends mostly on *doing*, at least for its outworking in physical matter. But doing that is not linked to being? We might as well be ants.

So what do we do? Well, from an earlier example, I assume you are into crystals rather than hubcaps, or you wouldn't have read this far.

Doing is the handmaiden of being, so wherever you are at in yourself right now, *do* something. Don't wait until you are a 'finished' person – you never will be. At least until the Universe completes itself. In 75 thousand million years or so.

Use your crystals to reflect back to you your most positive and harmonious attributes, and emphasize those. There is no need to put a lot of energy into your less harmonious ones – it just strengthens them. Remember:

energy follows thought
manifestation follows energy

The more you focus on something, the more you think about it, more energy you give it. How often do you draw to yourself what you fear the most? Fear is a powerful energy, thus has a powerful attraction. So work from your best attributes – focus on the positive, and that's what you will find.

Just sit with a crystal and love it for what it is. A little clear spot here, a little cloudiness there, a beautiful angle, a reflection of sunlight, a little chip off over there. However it is, it is perfect. Just like you.

Incidentally, to many people 'perfect' in crystals means unchipped and totally transparent. If you are one of those, I have a question for you: "If God is all things in the Universe, did he make that woebegone-looking crystal you are disdaining? If so, does he make anything that isn't perfect?"

Perhaps God has a different idea of perfection.

Or sit with your crystal, and attune to it. Then 'ask' it (remembering it is just reflecting you back), "How am I like you?", or "How am I not like you?" What you are really asking is "What is there in me that is Universal and whole?" and "What is there in me that is out of harmony with my own deepest nature?" The answers can be pretty surprising.

And if you feel like crying, then cry.

This exercise is best not practised on a No. 29 bus.

Also, don't judge your own progress by what appears to be progress in others. For the man who has a thousand miles to walk, a single step is not much. For a man on the edge of a cliff, a single step is a great deal. There is another circle-that-becomes-a-spiral:

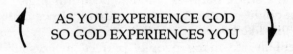

AS YOU EXPERIENCE GOD
SO GOD EXPERIENCES YOU

So, as you experience God, God experiences you ...

I've been talking about the learning experience of the Universe itself through this whole book. This is what it is all about, for me at least, as a human being.

We often talk about man being made 'in God's own image': the bearded old man on a celestial throne.

Thank God that image has more or less gone. That was really the root of the 'God is dead' movement of the sixties – the old image dying.

Okay, so what about God?

First, in my own mind, the words 'God' and 'Universe' are interchangeable. There are other ways of seeing it: 'God is the Mind of the Universe', or 'The physical Universe is the body of God.'

However you see it, we are still bound by the laws of energy. If you have an experience, so must everything else have an experience of you.

The Universe is a field of energy, existing at many different levels. But these are not *separate* levels. One level grades into the next, and there is a constant interchange between levels. If an experience occurs on one level, *all* levels have the experience, in accordance with their capacity.

That is another way of saying that *experiences occur on all levels anyway – it is only our limited perception that sees them on only one level.*

The spiral path of the Universe itself is its own expanding capacity for experience: for relationship.

Isn't this just like your own life?

An expanding capacity for relationship.

In the beginning, the Universe knew itself only as energy. If everything is the same, what is there to relate to? Nothing.

Many of you have experienced a similar state in deep meditation: that lovely floating feeling where everything is cozy and warm, and timeless. Your senses tell you a few minutes have gone by, and at the end of the meditation, your watch says it has been an hour.

What have you learned in that state?

If you think about it, not a lot. At least compared to being down here in the dirt being human.

What if you could go back in your own life to a similar state to that of the unformed Universe?

Assuming it were possible to survive, suppose you had been born in a totally dark, silent room, and instantly put into a totally dark, soundproof box, where you spent the next twenty years. No sound, no light, no human contact, *nothing.*

Do you suppose you would have any idea of who or what you were?

Remember the 'who you are not' circle? Doesn't your sense of identity come ultimately from what is reflected back to you from the world around?

Should it be any different for God?

If God experiences, then does God learn?

The laws of energy say *yes.*

But, if God learns, it means God doesn't know everything.

If the Universe *is* God, how *could* God know everything?

The Universe is not complete, not finished.

In fact, it's just beginning.

Remember, the Universe is still mostly hydrogen, even though all those stars are furiously making heavy stuff. How long will it take them to finish?

100,000,000,000,000 years.

Ten thousand times the current age of the Universe.

Give or take a few thousand million years.

If the Universe has in its plan for itself, the completion of that process, the using up of all of its hydrogen, then we can compare the current age of the Universe to your own lifetime.

It is about three hours old.

We, as human beings, have often seen ourselves as the bottom rung of spiritual evolution. Stuck down here in dense matter, with this heavy body to drag around, and-let's-get-enlightened-so-we-can-get-out-of-here. Back to the Spirit where we belong.

Wrong.

The Universe isn't going in that direction. It is moving into even *greater* density.

We aren't at the tag-end of spiritual evolution – *we are at its cutting edge.*

We aren't here to learn how to be God. At the inner level, we *already are.*

We are here to learn how to be *human.* How to relate at a dense level of being.

Without losing that inner sense of who we really are, and where we are really going.

Physical manifestation is part of the Universe's plan for discovering itself – for gathering experience through this incarnation of the Universe.

I feel sure that the Universe as a being replicates its own inner patterns – expansion and contraction. Birth – death – rebirth. In each incarnation of itself the Universe brings forward to its new incarnation all of the experiences of the last – the accumulation of every experience that has taken place in it.

There are only two choices for the Universe – expand forever, or expand to the point where gravity overcomes the momentum of expansion, and the Universe collapses back inward on itself, probably into another 'Big Bang' from the rebound.

We, in our own experience, choose a pattern that ultimately leads to Unity. The Universe, in choosing its pattern of incarnation, also chooses a series of interlocking patterns which also leads to Unity.

The Spiral Paths.

They look rather like the spirals on the next page.

Remember that the Universe too is bound by its own limitations. It cannot experience beyond its own capacity any more than you can.

So why does God create a Universe in the first place?

For the same reason you create your own body: as a vehicle for experience. To experience who and what you are. *To establish within yourself, the right relationship to all that exists.*

It is called LOVE.

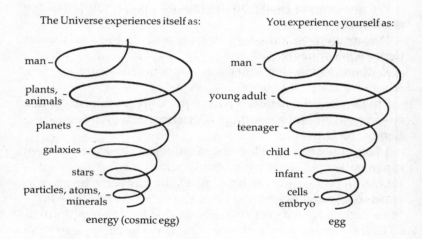

The Universe experiences itself as:

man –
plants, animals
planets
galaxies
stars
particles, atoms, minerals

energy (cosmic egg)

You experience yourself as:

man –
young adult
teenager
child
infant
cells
embryo

egg

Fig. 18

A last word: We live in a technological age – machines growing in complexity, as we once did. There is a lot of resistance to this in many 'spiritual' circles. Perhaps many are sensing the lack of consciousness that has gone into their creation.

But as long as we don't lose sight of our own creative power, the consciousness that has gone into creating it, what is wrong with technology? What is the difference between a wheelbarrow and a computer – except complexity. They are just different ways of arranging matter – putting matter into different relationships.

Aren't we just mimicking the Universe's own processes?

In the computer, we are creating complexity in essentially mineral matter, to give it intelligence – perhaps the next step will be to give it consciousness.

We are even at the stage of creating planets – we will call them space stations.

One last question remains? If we are, within our own lives, performing the activities of God, and are part of God's own experience of Himself, then *are we God?* The answer is up to you.

My sense tells me that God is all things that exist in the Universe. Man creates a dimension of this Being called God; and is an embodiment of that dimension which he creates. Man is not everything, and yet the essence of everything is in Man. Hu-man. = God-man.

Man and minerals, reaching for Unity.

The spiral goes on.

Notes

1. Carlo Rubbia, 'Worlds within the atom', *National Geographic*, (Vol. 167, No. 5, May 1985), p. 653
2. Fred Hoyle, *The Intelligent Universe* (Michael Joseph, London, 1983), p. 19
3. Lewis Thomas, *The Lives of a Cell* (Bantam 1974), p. 3
4. Thomas, p. 79
5. Thomas, p. 27
6. Thomas, p. 2
7. Thomas, p. 105, 106
8. Thomas, p. 12
9. Thomas, p. 13
10. J M Ziman, 'Information, Communication, Knowledge', *Nature*, (Vol. 224, 1969), p. 318-24
11. Thomas, p. 100
12. Thomas, p. 92
13. Thomas, p. 98
14. Thomas, p. 90

Bibliography

Dana, Edward S, *A Textbook of Mineralogy*, Wm E Ford, Ed., Fourth Edition, John Wiley & Sons, N.Y., 1932.

Hoyle, Fred, *The Intelligent Universe*, Michael Joseph, London, 1983.

Mason, Brian, *Principles of Geochemistry*, Second Edition, John Wiley & Sons, N.Y., 1958.

Sagan, Carl, *Cosmos*, Book Club Associates, 1980.

Smith, Elske & Jacobs, Kenneth, *Introductory Astronomy and Astrophysics*, W.B. Saunders Co., 1973.

Thomas, Lewis, *The Loves of a Cell*, Bantam, 1974.

Weinberg, Steven, *The First Three Minutes*, Flamingo, 1977, 1983.